Bridges
To A
Passionate Partnership

A Realistic Approach For Couples Who Want To Become Better Friends & Lovers

~

David LeClaire

EQUESTRIAN
PRESS

BRIDGES
To A
PASSIONATE PARTNERSHIP

A Realistic Approach For Couples
Who Want To Become Better Friends & Lovers

~

David LeClaire

HARA Publishing
P.O. Box 19732
Seattle, WA 98109

Cover Design: Brad Hale / Hale Design, Seattle, WA
Author Photograph: Charlotte Sara Oakes
The names used in this book are fictitious for privacy.

Printed in the United States of America

First Edition

ISBN 0-9651055-3-9

Library of Congress Catalog Card Number: 96-76383

LeClaire, David
   Bridges To A Passionate Partnership: A realistic approach for couples who want to become better friends and lovers / by David LeClaire
   1. Marriage.   2. Relationships.   3. Communication in marriage.   I. Title.

Copyright 1996

An Equestrian Press Publication

For Information On Quantity Purchases Call 1-800-905-1991

Acknowledgments

My deepest gratitude to my loving wife Kristin, whose love ignited a passion which I am grateful to have the opportunity to share. Thanks for all of your support, patience, and encouragement!

A special thanks To Brad Hale, Charlotte Sara Oakes, Vicki Berg, and all the others who graciously assisted in the development of this book.

Table Of Contents

~

*"Man can not discover new oceans until he has the
courage to lose sight of the shore."*
Unknown

~

CHAPTER 1

Bridges To A Passionate Partnership
Beating the odds by building a solid foundation

~

Consider the elements which are necessary for a bridge to be strong enough to withstand the forces of nature. First and foremost, a solid foundation must be put in place upon which the bridge can be safely built. Regardless of the design of the span, if the foundation is weak, the bridge will not be able to survive the test of time and the pressures it will be subjected to. The same can be said of a couple's relationship.

At the first signs of challenges or after a few half-hearted attempts at resolving their frustrations, too many people pack their bags and head for the door. The most important building block in a relationship's foundation is a "no matter what" commitment in which two people are truly partners for life.

Even couples who participate with "both feet in" will still face a variety of challenges in their life together. However, couples can take measures to reinforce and strengthen their foundation; helping them weather the storms and keep their love and respect for each other alive over the years.

Suzanne & Michael had gone for a long, relaxing weekend drive. After a fabulous dinner, they walked along the sandy beach to the sound of sea-gulls and crashing waves. They held hands and laughed as the sun set behind the scenic backdrop of the distant snow covered mountains. "I'm so lucky," Michael thought. "What a beautiful woman I've found. She understands me and believes in me. Suzanne has such a great attitude. I really love her."

Later that evening they were lying in bed together, enjoying the moment as they shared some of their favorite memories. For a while they laughed so hard their eyes became teary. Life was good. Michael held Suzanne in his arms, and she snuggled into his warm body. Suzanne let out a deep and peaceful sigh. It had been a long but wonderful weekend. She felt loved, safe, and truly happy. "Thank God I have him in my life," she thought.

Now the memory of that time together is faded and distant. The couple who "had everything" is standing in a lawyer's office, waiting to sign the papers that will legally terminate their marriage. Where did it go? What happened to the affection and respect that they both shared for each other? No one can deny that Suzanne and Michael had good times together once and that they genuinely loved each other. They were best friends, so how can they be waiting to revoke their vows and throw it all away?

Suzanne & Michael aren't "throwing it all away" because they *don't have the love, respect, and passion anymore.* They've lost their enthusiasm, their spontaneity, their patience, their understanding and compassion for each other. They've both lost their appreciation for their partner. All they have is faded memories of good times and vivid memories of the recent pain and frustration.

Now the pleasant moments are few and far between for Suzanne & Michael. Rare are the feelings of peace and calm from being with the one they love. What used to feel like their favorite pair of jeans has now become more like wearing a new pair of shoes that are much too small. Some may believe that they "should try more counseling" or "stay together for the kids," but the incentive to work it out is gone. If they both felt wanted, valued, appreciated, & loved, this may not be the case.

The reality is that this couple no longer possesses the inspiration to stay together because simply "working it out" will only amount to reaching some compromises and agreements. The love, the fun, and the passion would still be missing anyway.

Suzanne & Michael had a very weak foundation. When times were good at the beginning, they seemed perfect for each other. However, they didn't nurture their relationship, and allowed it to become a distant priority in both of their lives. As a couple they never learned to deal with conflicts. This led to resentments and frustration, which replaced their feelings of intimacy and love.

When challenges arose, they were not equipped to deal with them effectively, which resulted in driving them apart instead of pulling them together. Their friends were left saying things such as, "If one of them would have been around more," or "If they hadn't become so focused on their careers," or "If they had saved more time and energy for each other, they might still be in love." "If they could have just solved some of their conflicts with less hostility." "If they could have learned to communicate better." "If only ...." If, if, if.

Long-term relationships require a continuous effort and commitment

Many people mistakenly believe that if they find the right partner they will enjoy an effortless relationship. Others believe that marriage will transform a relationship into the magical bliss they dreamed of as a child. The reality is that once you find your partner for life the real work begins, not ends. However, this "work" doesn't have to be drudgery, but instead can be thought of as putting in energy and effort to maintain the love you've established.

If you were the proud owner of a beautiful new car, you would treat it well and have it washed and serviced regularly. Having your car's oil changed is no more "work" than taking a little time now and then to nurture and care for your relationship.

Long-term relationships can and do endure. The strong survive the challenges that can occur over the course of a lifetime. Those with a solid foundation will overcome the hurdles and avoid the obstacles that have taken a toll on many relationships.

Changes in lifestyle, attitude, finances, or even health can bring about situations that can weaken *or* strengthen a partnership. How a couple deals with the challenges is the true measure of the strength of a relationship. It's easy to be in love when everything is perfect. But this isn't a perfect world.

Just as there isn't one sole cause for the disintegration of relationships, there isn't one solution to keep all couples together. Is pursuing a "partnership for life" an exercise in futility as there are realistically just too many possibilities for failure? The answer is simply "No." Is there hope? Of course there is, although you may need to make adjustments and put in some effort. But it's worth it. Having a satisfying, passionate partnership is one of life's most rewarding experiences.

You may be asking, "What can we do? I don't want my life to look like Suzanne & Michael's." There are no magical potions or templates to follow that will guarantee your love will last. Yet there are simple and effective tools you can both use to create a strong foundation and build bridges to overcome obstacles that may appear in your lives.

Much of what is covered in the following pages is not highly technical or complicated. You may even find that particular topics and certain suggestions which are made simply reinforce what you already believe. While not every subject will be relevant to your life at the moment, I've tried to be fairly comprehensive in discussing some of the most "universal" issues. Yet, because relationships are so unique and different, not every possible aspect has been addressed.

This book is for couples who still love and respect each other, and who are truly interested in strengthening and enhancing their relationship. Those who have extremely serious problems will probably not find all of their answers and solutions here. While this book may be a valuable step in the right direction for such couples to take, it is not an adequate substitute for therapy, which is especially needed in situations such as abuse, alcohol or drug problems, etc.

The more a couple understands the dynamics of relationships and what has worked for other couples, the more possibility they have for surviving the challenges and keeping their love alive. You *can* live a long and happy life together. There are many positive steps you can take towards your goal of creating a fulfilling partnership rich with passion, respect, and affection, which you'll discover throughout this book.

Where Does Love Go?

The challenges you may face, including children, money, time, responsibilities, etc. do not in themselves end relationships. *Couples have learned how to navigate these areas successfully.* I believe that the most common reasons why the love and connection between a couple often deteriorates are:

1) Focus shifts to jobs, children, etc. & relationship is ignored
2) Inability to handle anger/conflicts with maturity and genuine forgiveness
3) Unrealistic expectations
4) Lack of trust which leads to possessiveness, jealousy, insecurities
5) Both people change and grow in different directions
6) Emotional barriers to being open, intimate, & loving
7) Lack of partnership & "team" attitude
8) Controlling person eventually drives their partner to seek freedom
9) One or both partners makes little to no effort to remain attractive, interesting, or enjoyable to be with
10) Couple originally married for the wrong reasons, and a strong foundation never existed

As time passes, a couple's relationship which suffers from one or more of the above situations may slowly deteriorate until little emotional incentive is left to try to fix their problems. Keep in mind that most people either don't recognize when they are in the middle of one these situations, or they simply don't know how to avoid or transcend these problems. Instead the loving attitude that brought them together turns to a hostile or resentful one. It is possible to reverse the direction a couple is heading together, although the longer they wait to make the necessary changes, the more difficult this task becomes.

Even though we know that to stay healthy we must eat right, exercise, and get plenty of rest, there are times in which most people neglect to follow this basic, timeless wisdom. Some of the ways to keep our relationships alive and thriving are also basic and simplistic. Yet we can and do make mistakes, from which we can also bounce back.

I believe having an intimate, long-term relationship may in fact be the most difficult undertaking most people will ever attempt in their lives. Getting along with another person, day by day, year after year, through thick and thin, can be challenging. You will have to deal with money, bills, sex, kids, careers, household duties, vacations, you name it. Yet many couples make it, affection and genuine love and appreciation for each other intact. This is possible for you too.

Love does not evaporate, fade, crack, chip, or peel on its own. Love between two people can slip away from them when they simply don't know how to do the dance together. You can learn how to recognize and avoid the traps and common problems that couples often face. By reading this book together you can continue building a solid foundation which will support your partnership for years to come.

How Strong Is Your Relationship Now?

By being honest with yourself, your answers to the following questions will give you a generalized assessment of some of your relationship's strengths and weaknesses. Each partner should take this assessment individually and record their answers on a separate sheet of paper. Compare your answers afterwards. Discuss the questions in which your scores were high as well as the areas in which your scores were quite different. This will give you some general ideas of some areas that may be of concern in your relationship.

Answer each question in regards to how frequently the statement applies to your relationship.

Never....0pt.s   Rarely....1pt   Sometimes....2pt.s   Regularly....3pt.s   Quite Frequently....4pt.s

1) Most of your free time is spent with friends or doing things without your partner

2) You sacrifice what you would like to do because you can't leave your children

3) You both stay home & rarely go out together to have fun

4) You have to ask (or be asked) to get help around the house with the housework, kids, etc.

5) You and your partner spend the majority of your time and energy talking about your careers and/or children instead of focusing on each other

6) One or both of you avoids your feelings by seeking satisfaction through drinking, drugs, or over eating.

7) When you have sex, even if pleasurable, you don't feel fulfilled

8) One of you seems to tune out the other, not really listening to what is being said

9) You are not together much because of work or busy schedules

10) One of you gets mad/hurt when you talk about sensitive issues

11) No matter how you do things, it never seems to be right or good enough for your partner

12) Forgiving isn't easy for you or your partner. One or both of you holds long-term resentment or grudges from past incidents

13) When you do get angry, it takes quite a long time to get past it before you are loving to each other again.

14) As a couple you argue about how to do things and get frustrated with each other

15) You and/or your partner complain about each other or criticize each other quite often.

16) When you are together it seems that often your partner says things that makes you feel he/she doesn't respect you

17) When you go to restaurants, long drives, or on vacation together, you don't have much to say to each other or end up getting into disagreements

18) You find yourself desiring, fantasizing, or flirting with people other than your partner

19) You share important feelings with friends about your partner because you can't discuss them with your partner since he/she won't listen or may become upset

20) There are subjects you avoid talking about re: your sex life

21) One of you neglects your appearance or personal hygiene and is no longer concerned about being attractive for the other

22) You or your partner feels taken for granted

23) One of you doesn't take the initiative to be intimate together

24) Your partner is controlling, giving you no freedom and demonstrating little trust or confidence in you

25) You know your relationship isn't terrible, but find yourself thinking it could be better

Count your individual total points. Which category on the following pages does your personal assessment of your relationship currently fall into?

0-40 points - Congratulations, your relationship is solid. Discuss the areas where there were higher scores or inconsistent answers with your partner. Reading this book will further strengthen your connection and foundation.

40-60 points - Caution, while your relationship is relatively healthy, you have some problem areas that could lead to even larger problems in the future. Discuss the warning signs of potential future challenges together. This book will help you come up with some solutions.

60-80 points - Your relationship is in a more advanced stage of trouble. While you will still benefit from reading this book, it would also be a good idea to look into counseling. Both of you must be committed to refurbishing your relationship and keeping the lines of communication open. You both will need to put in a significant effort to survive this.

80-100 points - Your relationship is in serious danger. While there is still a chance of saving it, you will probably not be able to do so on your own. You need a good counselor, and your success will require a strong mutual commitment and immediate action.

There Is More

It was a perfect day for golf. Tom and John were waiting for the foursome ahead of them to tee off. Even though they were good friends, they hadn't seen each other for a few months.

"So how's everything going with you and Sandy?" Tom asked. John thought for a few seconds, and then responded, "Pretty good I guess. We've been married for five years now, and we don't fight much. I suppose we're getting to understand each other better. I have to admit that sometimes I'm a little bored, and it's just not as fun as it used to be. It just seems like all we ever talk about anymore is our jobs and the kids. But overall it's not bad." Tom said, "I know the feeling. You know, it worries me that I find myself thinking about other women quite a bit lately. I love my wife, and we're doing all right. It just seems like a lot of the spark is gone."

Meanwhile, John's wife Susan was walking at a nearby park with Tom's wife, Marie. Susan said to Marie, "You and Tom seem to be so happy together. I don't know very many couples like you two. Are you really as happy as it looks?"

Marie responded, "You know Susan, we've got it pretty good. We have a nice house, great kids, and decent, well-paying jobs. I have a husband who I love and he loves me. When I was a little girl, this is everything I dreamed for. I tell myself I don't really have anything to complain about. Yet at times I feel lonely, and it seems like we're just going through the motions. It's the connection we used to have, that passion and enthusiasm for each other that seems so hard to hold onto. I feel like there must be more, but I don't think either of us knows how to get it."

Are you totally & completely happy with your relationship right now? Is there any room for improvement? If it's not bad, yet could be better, why not strive to add a little more passion, to have things run more smoothly, and to have more fun with each other?

Have you ever thought, "Is there more, and if so, how can we get it?" Would you rate your relationship as "pretty good," yet would like it to be great? Have you wondered what it will take to beat the odds and together keep your love alive? If you answered yes to any of these questions and you are truly interested in creating a life together you can both be proud of, then I'm confident you will find this book quite useful.

Believing In The Future

Maybe you're not certain you can make it, that you have what it takes. Forever is a long time - anything can happen. Do you hear a quiet but present ghost of a voice that asks, *"Why do you think you're so different?"* We all realize there are no guarantees. Yet you can take measures to keep your relationship healthy. It can and does work for some people, so why not try? Why not put forth the effort and give it your best shot. You *can* beat the odds, escape the "average" relationship pitfalls, and actually grow old together - happily.

Imagine an older couple sitting on a swing overlooking the beach. The sun is setting, and they're sipping on a glass of iced tea. Together they're laughing about the old times and all the stories that they created and participated in throughout their lives. The laughter is warming to anyone's soul. He reaches over and grabs her hand and tightly holds onto it as they smile and quietly look into each other's eyes for a moment. They still truly love each other after all these years.

It is possible. It does happen. And it can happen for you if you try. If you want it badly enough. If you consistently play to win throughout the majority of your lives. Do what it takes, including some compromise and openness to new ideas, throughout your partnership and life together. Show your partner that you care enough about him/her and about the two of you that you're willing to make the effort. There are many "bridges" to cross that will help you and your partner get to where you want to be together as a couple.

Take initiative to strengthen the foundation of your partnership, while you still care enough about each other and what you have. Continue on the course that you always wanted to be on. Who knows? You might find that it's the two of you who are someday sitting on that swing overlooking the ocean, smiling and laughing together about favorite memories as the sun sets.

~

CHAPTER 2

Teaching Old Dogs New Tricks

Expanding what's possible for you together

~

Each relationship is as different as the couple involved in it. Your relationship probably looks totally different than the couple's next door, yet both sets of partners may still feel happy and fulfilled. I believe in honoring and respecting the wide range of relationship possibilities rather than quibbling about the "right" way to do things or waste time trying to prescribe the formula for "perfect" relationships. Since every couple is different, obviously what two partners find important and the way they organize their lives will be their own unique definition of partnership.

Even though there may not be a template for couples to follow since we desire different things in our lives, a few important fundamentals are present in successful relationships. To begin with, expecting your partner to be everything to you is unreasonable. It's important for you to have friends, jobs, or individual interests and activities in order to have the experiences and life you want. Many times men or women want their partners to share all of their interests, or become frustrated when their partner doesn't interact with them as their girlfriends or buddies would.

Allowing each other to have the freedom and flexibility to be individuals is also important to the longevity of the relationship. Too many people try to change in whatever manner their partner desires in order to try to please them, and along the way they lose themselves and their self-expression. Others create an imbalance in the relationship by trying to control their partner. While a person may put up with this for a while, many come to resent "living someone else's idea of a life."

Even simpler than these two examples are the timeless truths that have persisted throughout countless generations. The "basics" are just as important now as they were to your grandparents, although we may interpret them differently today. Successful relationships consist of: compatibility, friendship, intimacy, affection, love, and passion.

Both partners seek to show understanding, forgiveness, appreciation, respect, support, and teamwork. Couples who have such a bond are also patient, caring, honest, trusting, sharing and generous. Time has not and will not change the importance of these fundamentals. Yet, to many people, having such a relationship seems beyond their grasp.

Unfortunately too many people settle for less than they can have in a relationship because they don't believe that what they want is either possible, realistic, or important enough.

Many of the "basics" to which I've just referred are woven throughout this book as they relate to couple's differences, conflicts, communication, intimacy, and partnership. While having a "perfect" relationship may not be possible day in and day out, it is certainly possible to experience a life together in which many of these basics are present *most* of the time. When you fail or come up short in one of these important areas, recognize and acknowledge your short-comings and strive to improve towards creating the partnership you want.

Give yourself a break for being human and for life being imperfect. Don't allow yourself to wallow in disappointment or guilt when you come up short. Committing to improvement gives you the drive to not settle for less than you and your partner deserve.

What does life look like when the basic fundamentals are present? You have a companion with whom you can spend your days comfortably and in peace. As a result of being together, you are both better people. You both have someone you *enjoy* waking up with, having breakfast with, talking with throughout your day, and spending quality time with during evenings and weekends. Together you have fun going on adventures and vacations. You would have a *companion* who you passionately love, appreciate, enjoy, and respect, who also feels the same way about you. Very few people experience these positive results of a relationship for an extended period of time.

If asked what the most important elements of a relationship were, the majority of people would surely come up with many of the same answers. However, they might define or prioritize these elements differently. One might say that good sex was the most important thing in a relationship. Sex can be enjoyable, but what you really need out of sex is the intimacy and a powerful connection with another human being. You may experience this connection in a very intense manner through sex, but in the end, it's still the intimacy that men and women are after.

Someone else may say communication is the most important part of a relationship. To be more accurate, effective communication is one of the most important *tools* that a couple can have and use in order to build and maintain their connection and intimacy. Others may think that humor and fun is the most important "part" of a relationship. But this again is only the result of the rapport, friendship and companionship, not the cause of it.

Yes, it is that acceptance, love, and bond with another human being that is underneath all of our relationship pursuits. It helps to be clear what we're after, what stands in our way to getting it, and how to get around the obstacles. There is no reason why you can't have everything that a great relationship can offer. It is possible to get the basic elements out of a relationship that you want, need, and deserve.

What Changes Are Realistic?

The serenity prayer used in some recovery groups is especially relevant: "God, help me change the things I can, accept the things I can't, and give me the wisdom to know the difference."

Can you teach old dogs new tricks? The answer depends on whether the dog wants to learn new tricks or not. Young puppies are typically energetic and eager to please, and thus easier to train. Older dogs are often more relaxed & lazy, and have an established lifestyle that doesn't include a lot of "new" learning. Obviously, a dog that has been learning new tricks all of it's life will usually continue to be easy to train regardless of its age.

How is this analogy relevant to people? When in a new relationship, people may be more open and willing to change because they still have the enthusiasm and desire to please their partner. If a person has been in the mode of growing, changing, and pro-actively seeking learning throughout most of their life, regardless of how old they are, they can easily learn new "tricks" as well. The most challenging are people who think they have done it all, know it all, and in actuality haven't been open to growth for many years.

Unless such a person has a major "incentive" to change, they probably won't. Many older couples figure that learning about relationships is a waste of time at this stage of the game. They "know" there is no way their partner is going to change after all of these years. Yet it can happen. However, when both partners buy into this belief, they create a self-fulfilling prophecy. This misguided belief is based upon their knowledge of their partner from years of experiences together.

While one can't deny the past, the future is yet to occur. If a couple is bored, lonely, frustrated, or disappointed enough, they *can* change. Unfortunately, at this point in their lives, most have settled into a resigned state of mind, having decided what life is and will always be for them.

What kind of change is realistic? Surely not everyone can "reinvent" themselves just because they or someone else wants them to. Most of our core beliefs are pretty solid and unshakable. For example, try to change a Republican into a Democrat, or a Catholic into a Jehovah's Witness. Try to get a laid-back person to become a driven, motivated, and relentless workaholic. It probably won't happen. Our personalities and values are relatively firm and often hard to change.

Behaviors, attitudes, and perspectives are what can be changed at any age. For example, a person can learn to become a better listener. A woman can learn to not "mother" her husband so much. A man can learn to show more respect and appreciation for his wife.

Attitudes usually change as the result of new "learning." As a man and woman begin to understand the opposite gender more, their expectations and attitudes may change towards each other. Consequently, the way they interact with their partner often changes. Their appreciation and respect for each other grows. They may not change in personality, but can change in the way they look at life, the way they see each other, and the way they interpret the situations around them. Couples who read this book may very well experience a shift in their attitudes and perspective, which can bring new life and passion into their lives.

*By leaving the door open to the possibility that you can
learn something new, you can change at any age.
Many long-term relationships have been revived
simply as the result of shifts in attitudes.*

Shaping A Partnership

Almost every relationship has some room for improvement. When some of the initial excitement fades, you may bump into some uncomfortable obstacles together. Those who do not possess a firm commitment may be quick to abandon ship in the search for an easier path or the perfectly harmonious relationship that will be exciting forever. Yes, people and relationships do change over time. Yet with determination and some practical and effective tools, you and your partner can grow closer and learn how to get even better at doing this dance together.

A lot of people know what makes a satisfying relationship, and they understand the fulfillment a healthy relationship can bring. Still, many of these same people never are fully committed to seeing that their relationship is just that. Sometimes life is no different than the movies and novels which are full of loving husbands or wives who are ignored or mistreated by their busy or passionless partner. While they are sad or depressed about it, they often never take a stand for what they deserve.

There are people everywhere who have never taken their needs, wants, and desires seriously enough to do whatever it takes to feel fulfilled in their lives, including the area of relationships. Instead they "go through the motions," some in constant conflict, others simply just tolerating each other. Some start with what seems like the answer to their prayers and dreams, only to see it slowly fade and slip away. It doesn't have to be this way.

Since we can't buy a pre-packaged relationship, we must recognize and acknowledge that we create and shape our partnerships. Take the reins and assume responsibility for the way your relationship unfolds and plays out, and begin steering it in the direction that will lead to more mutual satisfaction. Read this book *together* and begin to charter a course.

Whether you have a partnership that is also a marriage or not, the truth remains that it takes a team, both people, to keep it together and to make it work. This must be maintained by a *mutual* commitment.

The commitment must be continually reinforced by love, respect, appreciation, and all of the other positive results you need to get out of a relationship. When you don't get the benefits that a good relationship can provide, when you don't get what you deserve, want, and need from your partner, naturally the desire to put forth the effort & energy dwindles.

Many good, solid, relationships are prematurely abandoned because they have either grown stale or one partner doesn't get enough out of it. If they only knew *how* to inject some life into their partnership or were able to alter their current way of doing the dance together many couples could have their relationship be passionate and fulfilling again.

Two people who truly love each other can create a relationship where both people get almost everything they want and need. You can and do have the power to shape relationships to be like you want them to be.

A relationship is exactly what two people make it. You can consciously set out to create a partnership that works for both people. Even after many years together, couples can remodel or redesign their relationship to fit their current needs, wants, interests, and desires. Nothing is truly set in stone. I've personally seen transformations in relationships of people of all ages. Regardless of how far into it you are, whether you are young and just beginning, or retired and set in your ways, you can adjust who you are with your partner. You can have a dramatically improved experience of what a relationship is for both of you.

In his 70's, my father began to notice my mother aging and became determined to be the husband he felt he never was to her. After forty years of marriage their relationship has changed because he wanted it to badly enough. He truly shows her the love, respect, and appreciation that she deserves, which is moving to anyone who has known them over the years.

Sometimes one person must initiate the changes even though there are no guarantees their partner will follow their lead. Clearly the best situation is where both partners are willing to inquire into how they can become even better partners for each other, and look to find how they can strengthen and enhance their relationship.

Many people live average lives and maintain average relationships because they are either lazy, afraid to try new things, arrogant and think they know it all, or have no idea how to get to where they want to be from where they currently are.

Obviously you must be a person who cares about how your life turns out and must be open-minded and willing to change since you have picked up this book. You can learn how to breathe more energy, passion, enthusiasm, and commitment into your relationship. By reading further, I guarantee you will find practical and relevant ways to shape your partnership into what you both desire and deserve in your lives.

Getting What You Deserve

What you believe you deserve is probably all that you will have in your life. Of course you could be one of the few, one of the lucky, who somehow magically has great things fall into their laps. But the majority out there get what they think and feel they deserve. This is particularly true in relationships. When one's self-image is such that they believe they don't have much to offer, they often in turn hold low expectations for what kind of partner they can draw, or what they expect from the partner they have.

Many single people have asked me, "Why do I keep meeting and getting involved with losers?" The answer is simple. They subconsciously believe the good ones wouldn't be interested. I once heard someone say it's not that a person keeps meeting losers, it's that they keep giving them their phone number! If instead a person felt they were worthy and deserved more, they would hold out for it.

Others have asked me, "Why does my husband or wife treat me the way they do?" I believe that's because they have conditioned them over a period of time to believe it's OK to do so. Absurd? Certainly not. By tolerating and accepting patterns of behavior over long periods of time, we in fact "train" our partner how they can treat us.

How you build your self-esteem is a relatively complex subject in itself, and there are other books and resources to refer to for those that need some help in this area. However, the basis of one's impression of themselves is still quite relevant.

Your *self-image* is based upon how you see yourself and how you believe others see you. You make judgments upon yourself based upon your comparison between who you think you could/should be to who you think you actually are. This has much to do with your *self-esteem*, which is how you *feel* about yourself. Your self-esteem is based upon what you think you are and are not capable of, and your beliefs regarding your assets and limitations.

The inner-workings of your mind are complex and interwoven. The science of psychology is simply the study of how a person's thinking shapes their emotions and behaviors. Your thoughts about yourself are related to a myriad of messages you have received over the years, from yourself and others. It's a bigger subject than can be squeezed into a small chapter here. Basically, your thoughts can and do shape your actions. And your impression of what you're worth will have an impact on what you decide you can accept and what you should settle for.

This fundamental reality goes much further than simply who you choose as a partner. It is woven and laced into all aspects of your relationship with this person. When someone feels they are being ignored, mistreated, taken for granted, or disrespected, what do they do about it?

People who have high self-esteem or a good, healthy impression of themselves typically let their partner know that changes need to be made, and they will not just accept empty promises. They require and expect change. This doesn't need to be done with a demanding or authoritative tone, but instead can be a non-confrontational and firm statement that relates the message that they're serious.

Those with low self-esteem either put up with an enormous amount of frustration without saying anything, or they'll say something, complain, or become upset, but don't "require" follow-through. Instead they allow their partner to continue without changing, and do nothing to have their needs met.

After a while, your partner learns what they can and can't get away with based upon what you allow them to do. It's not much different than the testing that goes on between children and their parents. Most of us may not "test" our partners on purpose, yet through a series of experiences, incidents, and time, we find out what the rules or boundaries are. We learn how our partners feel about themselves, and get a sense for their self-esteem, and how we must treat them.

We also get clues about how we must treat our partner based upon how they treat themselves. The person who takes care of themselves, eats well, is healthy, and exercises makes a statement about how important their body is to them. We tell others that we don't respect ourselves very much if we continually become run down and sick. If we let our bosses or jobs dictate how much time we can spend with our spouses or children. If we don't show that we have boundaries, that we are important and deserve to be treated in a certain manner, then we tell those in our lives they can get by with mistreating us as well.

If you truly believe that you are an incredible human being, that you have a lot to offer, that you're interesting, caring, and worthwhile, you must show this by the manner in which you treat yourself, and how you let people treat you. If you can do this in a non-egotistical manner, in a way that says, "I'm not arrogant but I firmly believe that I have a lot of value," you will see many good things come into and flourish in your life. The alternative is years of disappointments and frustration, and you will settle for a lot less than you actually deserve.

We all need to take responsibility for getting what it is that we want. Don't wait for someone to just give everything to you. Victims are those who have things happen to them. They believe themselves to be "powerless" to do anything about all of the misfortunes that come their way in life. You can bet most "victims" are typically low in self-esteem.

A lot of unhappy people in relationships are not assertive. They bite their tongues or ignore what they want because they think it's unreasonable. They say to themself, "It's asking too much. I won't get it anyway. I'm not worth it. I won't find anyone better than this. This is just what I get. I might as well not get upset about it. Oh well, life could be worse." We could talk all day about effective communication, but if a person doesn't believe they're worth much, they won't use what they know about communication anyway.

Look for ways to boost your perception of yourself if you think your current analysis of yourself is low. If you don't believe your perception of yourself is low, and yet you're unhappy with circumstances in your life, then look at the messages you send out to those around you. If you're unhappy, there's a good chance that it is because you are allowing it to be so, and allowing others to give you less than you need or deserve.

You and I are both worthy of having the best life has to offer. We can learn how to create it. You deserve to be listened to, to be respected and appreciated. You deserve affection, love, and all of the positive things that a great relationship can offer. You must not only agree and believe this, but take the appropriate actions and measures to bring it and keep it in your life. Remember, old dogs can learn new tricks. Challenge yourselves and strive to expand what's possible in your relationship.

~

"It is difficult to love those whom we do not esteem,
but it is no less difficult to love those whom we esteem
much more than ourselves."
La Rochefoucauld, Maxims, 1665

CHAPTER 3

The Mirror
What kind of partner have you been lately?

~

Spying On You

In the beginning of new relationships, most of us present our best attributes to potential partners. We're understanding, sympathetic, and forgiving. We laugh more, initiate more activities to share together, and maintain a relatively happy disposition. We're more interested & more interesting, with energy and a natural willingness to help.

If the potential relationship catches, over time many of our wonderful attributes seem to slowly erode away. Is this inevitable? Of course not. Is it common? Absolutely. We *can* keep ourselves interesting and our relationship fresh. The challenge is being able to recognize when we've changed and are no longer the wonderful person that we initially were when we first became involved.

If you have been in a relationship for at least a few years, try taking a look at your life and what you're offering your partner from the eyes of someone else.

Imagine that Life Magazine was doing a feature story on current relationships in America. They needed to find couples that would be good examples of our culture. They sent people to look in the windows of households across America, and without knowing it, your neighborhood was selected.

Unbeknownst to you, last week everything you did in your home was watched by a reporter. He saw you get up in the morning and go to bed at night. He listened to your conversations over meals, on the phone, and during your private times together. For one whole week he saw each of you as the partner you were really being - not as the partner you *think* you are.

The reporter had a checklist with items such as: How patient were you? How much appreciation for each other did you share? Did you have energy or were you a lump on the couch? How intimate and affectionate were you? He was also looking to see if you helped your partner with the little things, if you were listening when they talked to you, if you were fun to be around, or were you instead annoying, picky, insulting, lazy, or demeaning?

Your neighbors Jack and Diane were also selected. Here's what the reporter had to say about Jack:

"Jack is a handsome, successful executive. He is charming, witty, well-dressed, and very courteous. Most of the women he encounters are charmed by him. But don't be fooled by his image. After watching Jack with his wife for a week, it was easy to see that he isn't really everything you might imagine."

"As a partner, Jack is rarely there for his wife. He routinely seemed to tune her out, and was even demeaning towards her attitudes, opinions, and feelings throughout the week. When it came to helping out around the house, he did manage to change the toilet paper roll once. He was impatient when his wife didn't understand how to do things, and demanding about how the household duties were performed."

Jack's review continued. "Sure, he's successful. But his commitment to success is merely a reflection of his overwhelming focus on himself. He spent little time with his wife or family, and was only partially present when they were together. At the end of the day, Jack routinely buried himself in his work or the TV, and only during commercials or bathroom breaks could anyone interact with him."

"When his wife put together a beautiful dinner, Jack read the Wallstreet Journal throughout the meal, talked business, and complained that the meat was dry. When they went to bed, this beautiful man who flirts all day with women was as passionate as a park bench."

"After one week, we concluded that Jack is the picture of a great catch, but once reeled in, someone choosing him for a partner will probably find he's not the fish they thought they had on the line. Unfortunately, Jack seems to closely resemble the profile of many who we've documented during this study."

What would the review say if it was about you? If you were being critiqued last week how would you have scored? If asked to assess yourself and compare your rating with that of an unbiased observer, chances are your scores wouldn't be too close. Our own self-assessments are rarely very adequate.

What are you really like from the other people's perspectives? Although your partner is not totally unbiased, they do see you through an entirely different set of eyes than how you see yourself. When you are whining or complaining, when you are unappreciative or impatient, they are watching. Sure, your partner isn't Life Magazine, but their perspective is actually more important.

We typically think we're wonderful,
and when we aren't, it's usually not our fault.

Most of the time we rationalize away our actions,
failing to take responsibility for them.

Your partner is the person you are committed to living your life with You're spending much of your energy and a significant part of your life with this person. What they see, what they observe, and what they experience is what is truly important, not what you *think* you are offering.

There is typically a major difference between the person you may think you are and the reality of who you really are. If someone was spying on you, what would they conclude? By listening to your partner's perspective, you will discover a few clues about how you have changed or may need to.

Because it's easier to point our fingers than to change ourselves, divorce eventually becomes a reality for one out of every two couples. When we are aware of our shortcomings and are committed to growth and improvement, we can consciously charter a course of action and work towards being the kind of partner we would like to say we are.

The Winning Formula

Most people see life as an uphill struggle, and hope to get to a plateau where they can rest. We fantasize about kicking back and everything will be handled from there on. We'll have the "winning formula" that allows us to coast and watch the system we developed take care of everything.

Unfortunately there is no such plateau, there is no coasting. It's all an imaginary goal that we never really can reach similar to the pot of gold at the end of the rainbow. For example, even if we get rich, we'll be afraid of losing it or instead worried about our health, our appearance, or yes, our relationships. The challenges don't end, they just change.

Life is to be lived, not watched from a distance
with a remote in our hand.

Yet, because it's human nature, or maybe more accurately our "American" nature, we still strive to devise the winning formula. Because there is no universal "right" way for everything, we end up devising our own formula based upon our own experiences and lessons learned. We decide that whatever success we've attained thus far is the result of our own personal winning formula, and from there try to apply this formula to future challenges, projects, and situations in our lives.

Most of us look for patterns to follow that will make our lives easier,
more efficient, with less work and struggle.

Many strive to "figure it all out." They hope life's complexities
will become simple, including their relationships. But relationships are
fluid and ever-changing, made up by individuals who are also constantly
changing. This makes creating the perfect system and having all of the
answers impossible. Continually learning and adapting is essential to
succeeding in a long-term relationship. Those that figure they know it
all and have the winning formula are unsuspectingly walking across a
sheet of thin ice.

"It is not true that life is one damn thing after another.
It's the same damn thing over and over again."
Edna St. Vincent Millay

Life as an adult, especially in an urban atmosphere, is typically
busy and complicated. With many things that you're trying to do at once,
in order to keep them all running, you juggle your energy, attention,
time, and efforts.

When a crisis occurs, you are forced to reprioritize in order to put
out the fire. For example, while not intentionally, sometimes people let
their health take a back seat. Then at the age of 45 or so they have a heart
attack or a serious health problem, and suddenly have to shift some of
their attention and energy to their health.

Many adults move from one area of crisis to another, because
balancing everything in life has become quite difficult. Keeping on top
of the bills, being involved with your family, keeping the yard under
control, staying healthy and active, and sharing time with friends can be
challenging. Having a full time job is a full time job.

Add to the equation keeping your relationship in good operating
condition, and you indeed do have a balancing act. Life just keeps getting
more complicated, so we strive to develop systems that can make handling
all of this possible. But no system is perfect, and inevitably, things fall
through the cracks.

The "Slump"

Since people often think they've found the winning formula for their relationship, they move on to the other areas that still require much effort and attention, such as their children or careers. They slip into a rut, not really noticing that they're leaving little or no energy for their partner. Without a continued effort, care, and focus, like a house plant, the relationship will eventually wither and die. While it may not be easy juggling all of your concerns, it is possible.

Most of us want to have a solid relationship, a satisfying and well-paying job, and a home that we enjoy. Not everyone strives to make a ton of money, have a flock of kids, a big home, or take exotic vacations. But almost every healthy, normal person eventually wants to have a companion and lover in their life. When the relationship piece is in place, it can make the other pursuits easier to work at and focus on.

The squeaky wheel is often what gets the most attention.

Once we've found our partner and established a winning formula together, people naturally move on to other "squeaks." After all, our other interests and goals are important too.

Imagine you're happy and find renewal and comfort in the partnership that you have. If a loud squeak comes from your financial situation, or the needs of your children, it is easy to redirect your focus to that area. Eventually, regardless of your intentions to not ignore your relationship, you will probably do so from time to time. People figure why worry about it, especially when there's no immediate crisis? Our attention is needed in other areas instead. While that may be true, a strong partnership is one where the attention comes back to the relationship without too long of a hiatus. Too many partners get off track and never seem to get back on again.

Too many times we don't dedicate enough energy and focus on our relationship, even though it is one of the truly most important things in our life. Many adults travel all the time, work late almost every night, or become totally consumed by the needs and interests of their children. As a result their partner gets an exhausted, lifeless person when they finally shut off their business or parental mind. Or they get the heap of a person planted in front of the tube with whom conversation is almost non-existent throughout the evening. Once in bed, they quickly fall asleep. Only when their relationship starts showing visible, serious signs of neglect do some wake up and notice. Even then, for some people, the pain is not that great, and they take no measures to remedy the situation. Many wait too long, while the problem slowly grows out of control. This does not have to be the path you follow. You can be more preventative. You can stay focused on your relationship even though you have all of these other interests and areas of concern.

Many of Darren's friends insisted they wanted to be single. Yet they would spend an enormous amount of time in bars, going on dates, and thinking about the different "possibilities" around them at places such as the mall and the gym.

Darren was also a typical single guy. Being single was fun for a while - but like his friends who appeared to enjoy it, he secretly longed to find that "connection." One of the most important goals for him was to find a partner. Darren put a significant amount of his energy into establishing a new partnership. Tired of coming close but finding just one too many pieces missing, Darren passionately wanted to find and be with "the one."

When Darren found Angela, he didn't immediately lose his energy for doing things. He remained an active, enjoyable person to be with. After all, he had to keep this potential partners interest, and since it was fun anyway, why not?

The pursuit of everything that Darren always wanted suddenly seemed to be within his grasp. He'd been waiting to find a successful rhythm in life, where he would have a great partner and family, a solid income, a satisfying lifestyle, etc. Darren found the right partner and couldn't be happier. Life was good. After having been to the bars and on so many dates, he was glad he didn't have to "do all that anymore." Darren and Angela looked forward to the peaceful tranquillity of being with someone they loved. Like most of us, he wanted to eventually be able to relax and not worry about tomorrow.

Our life starts becoming intertwined with our partner's, and we become companions and best friends. We learn each other's habits, and make up our own inside jokes and phrases with secret meanings that only our partner understands. We fall asleep in each others arms with a smile on our face, and look forward to the rituals we establish. Whether it may be lying on the couch watching a movie together, going out for coffee on Saturday mornings, or whatever the pattern - we look forward to doing "our favorite things."

Most of us have experienced how fun a new
relationship can be at the beginning
when you are excited and hopeful about the "potential."

Most people long for this peace. To have the person we love next to us when we wake up in the morning, to walk with us on a beach at sunset, and to cuddle up with on the couch on a cold winter night. The fallacy is that our life will be perfect once we find this partner. Together, other than a few bumps in the road, we think we'll be forever happy with the person in our life with whom we've developed a familiar, comfortable, and satisfying pattern. The indisputable truth is that not everything in life will be perfect just because we have each other.

The nest gets built, and everything seems to be in place. And it is, for a while. Because people strive to attain "comfort," we are temporarily quite content. Yet humans are also fickle creatures, and after a while get tired of even the best things. And so, the pattern that we love which became like our favorite pair of shoes - wears out. One day we look at those ratty old shoes and face the fact that they're tattered.

Quite often in our relationships someone eventually looks around at the "pattern" and decides they're bored. Partners become so comfortable with each other that they no longer feel the appreciation like they used to. They long to have their partner want to make love to them passionately. They want to take those long walks with someone and talk for hours about everything under the sun. They're officially in a *"slump."* And so, this rhythm, this system, this pattern that we wanted so badly, can eventually turn into boredom.

Angela looks at her husband Darren lying on the couch with the remote in his hand. He hasn't moved for and hour and a half much less changed expressions. Darren looks at Angela. She's wearing baggy clothes, her hair looks wild, and she's wearing no make up. He looks back at the glamour model on "Baywatch," barely hearing Angela say she's going to bed She lies there alone, remembering the days they used to go to bed together and make love on a consistent basis.

Darren and Angela aren't fighting with each other, there's no major crisis in their lives. But the zing is gone, the pow, the punch. The familiarity has slowly worn down the sharp edges to the extent that it has become dull. So many relationships die because of this need for "stimulation," for change, for variety. What's the solution? It's simple. Keep it interesting.

When you see yourself entrenched in patterns that don't seem to change, try something different. It's almost like waking up. You can get this fresh look at your life without starting over with a new partner. But it must start from within.

Leaving your partner isn't going to make *you* more interesting. The only reason you would become more interesting if you were to start over is because you would have to, since most people wouldn't be intrigued by someone in a slump.

The slump happens to almost everyone, men and women, young and old. It's our nature to try to get things set up so we can kick back, but the inherent danger is that it will get boring. So every once in a while we must wake ourselves up, shake ourselves, get clear about who we really want to be, and recommit to being that person, to being more alive.

Chances are, if you're bored, you've probably been pretty boring also.

There is no guarantee that by dusting yourself off and doing a little polishing that your partner will respond in a similar manner. But when you notice that you're in some kind of a slump, try to snap out of it for yourself, for your own pride, if for no other reason.

*Ask yourself, "How would the person in my life see me
if I was just beginning to get to know them?"*

*"Am I the kind of person I would be if I was single
and looking to find a partner?"*

Get up off the couch and do something different. Throw a curve
ball in your life; be outrageous. Reclaim your youthful energy, and strive
to avoid the rut. This is possible, and easy to do, *if you can see the slump.*
If you can't see it you'll have no incentive to do anything differently.

One of the dangers is that sometimes you don't see it, but it hits
your partner head-on. Remember, if your partner feels there is a slump,
whether you agree or not, you better deal with it as if there *is* a slump.
Your partner's perception of a problem is all it takes, regardless of what
you want to believe.

Relationships die around us everyday, and many of them do not
fall prey to arguments and hostility, to affairs, to bankruptcy, or whatever.
They often slip, quietly and subtly, into this state of boredom and become
stale. If you experience a slump, it doesn't mean you are with the wrong
person, or the relationship has "died," or that you need to abandon ship.
You just need to learn how to revive yourself once in a while. If you look
in the mirror and see that you could be much more alive, passionate, and
energetic, why not rise to the occasion and become the person and partner
you know you can be.

No one ever said it shouldn't be this way, that it won't ever get
old or ever become boring. But you and I are not powerless. We don't
have to sink into the quagmire of the painless but lifeless slump! We can
do something about it if we choose. Reclaim that passion for living and
share it with your partner. It can be contagious. It's your life. Do it for
yourself if for no other reason.

~

*"Many persons have a wrong idea of what constitutes
true happiness. It is not attained through self-gratification
but through a fidelty to a worthy purpose."*

Helen Keller

CHAPTER 4

Quicksand or Trampoline?

Simple lessons for avoiding "the slump" that couples can fall into

~

Energy

So how do you break out of a slump and reclaim that passion for living? How do you put more life into your relationship? The bridge to having more life in your relationship is changing your attitude. *Live with an attitude that is enthusiastic and positive.* When you're truly excited to be alive, the results become contagious, and effect all of the elements of your life, including work, friendships, your health, and of course, your relationship.

Obviously the philosophy of "think positive" is unrealistic at times. Our lives have too many ups and downs, too many victories and disappointments, to be able to stay in one frame of mind all of the time. Yet it's important to find a way to recover and bounce back quickly from life's difficulties, which is made possible from a change in your attitude or perspective.

Find ways to experience significantly more pleasure than pain on a daily basis. Look for areas that you want to change and set a plan to do so. For example, if you seem to regularly be low on energy, look at your lifestyle, diet, and other habits that can be changed. Actually being happy, energetic, and passionately alive *is a skill.*

Instead of asking people how they're doing,
ask them if they're excited to be alive today.
Unfortunately you probably won't find many genuine yes's.

People who are enthusiastic and enjoying life are not only more fun to be in a relationship with, but are typically healthier and more inspiring to around. Do you complain often and spend a lot of energy on things that frustrate or annoy you? Or do you try to keep the negativity in your world a small part of your consciousness and focus more on the other aspects of life? Remember, when you aren't happy, it's harder to get excited and stay motivated for anything.

You may find it interesting that many psychologists believe depression is often simply an energy crisis. People who aren't excited about anything and are focused on the negativity in their lives often have little or no energy.

Relationships which seem to be in a slump aren't always made up of depressed or negative people. On the contrary, many who are "in a slump" are actually very active in their careers, activities, or child-rearing. Yet their daily life *as a couple* usually becomes boring and provides nothing to get excited about. Eventually many of these couples find their life *together* has become routine, uninteresting and they rarely leave any energy for each other.

Even the fortunate couples who are truly great together can occasionally get in a slump and take things for granted for a while. Unintentionally, we can begin living on "auto pilot" and become numb. The first step to getting out of a slump is to catch yourself in one, and the earlier the better. Don't be hard on yourself if you do find you're in a slump; recognize it and move forward!

The next step is acknowledging how the slump you're in is costing you. Does it ever feel like you're sinking into the quagmire of routine or dragging around a ball and chain? What are you giving up or how could life be even better for you? Visualize what your life would or could be like. Last and most important, *commit to taking specific actions that will shake things up and then follow through.* Remember, each of these pieces are essential.

Richard and Melanie are living in a small suburb outside of Philadelphia. When they met he was a successful corporate lawyer, she a respected pediatrician. They enjoyed their life together immensely. They had the resources to take adventures together, and did. Richard and Melanie often played racquetball and went sailing and skiing. They loved to go to a local jazz club and out to eat. Since they were having so much fun as a couple, they got married and "settled down." Five years ago it seemed they were at the pinnacle of life.

In the past few years they've told themselves they were just too busy for going on adventures together. Yet they were just as "busy" when they first met. Most of their activities were shelved, rationalized by telling themselves, "It's only temporary." The reality was they hadn't gone on an adventure together in over two years, and they weren't doing any of their favorite activities either. They still loved each other, but it was just too easy for them to use the excuse of being "too busy." Melanie confided in me, "I'm afraid we may be falling into the trap that so many couples get into. We have little energy left for each other at the end of the day. We rarely do things together anymore, and often we end up just reading or watching TV."

Melanie and Richard had to redesign parts of their daily lives. Now they actually plan ahead for time to have fun. Now they schedule dinners and activities, and set aside time to go on adventures together. They both realized that they had become a little too serious about work and making money for "someday." Today they are more like the couple they were when they met, but it has taken a conscious effort and an ongoing commitment on both of their parts.

Most people don't see the slump or hear their partner's comments about the boredom until it's too late. Unfortunately it occasionally takes a drastic move such as moving out or filing for divorce before some partners may wake up. Yet you can live an exciting, fulfilling life and avoid many of the negative consequences others have experienced by *choosing to have more energy& keeping your life together interesting!*

Many actually see the slump but only make a half-hearted attempt to get out of the trance. After one spontaneous burst of energy or doing a few things different for a while, they slip back into the old routine. Following through and making a continued effort is essential. The only way follow through will occur is when there is an underlying commitment that can support taking consistent actions over a period of time. How committed are you to avoiding living your life in a boring routine? How strongly do you feel about being an energetic and enjoyable partner?

Energy is one thing you cannot buy. It can't be given to you.

The source of energy is actually within you.
You must be able to call up energy at will,
just like an athlete must in order to go the distance
once they begin to feel exhausted.

Knowing this gives you access to suddenly springing off the couch even when you *believe* you have no energy left. Try it. The next time you're lying on the couch and catch yourself thinking, "I'm so tired, I don't want to get up," suddenly jump to your feet, for no reason, other than to prove that you can call up this energy at will if you need to. Part of your energy level is the result of your thinking, which can be changed more easily than you may believe.

Of course, remember that relaxation is also important, as is balance and moderation. When most couples begin to date, they usually have an abundance of energy to experience things together. Over time, this energy often shifts to careers or children. If you find that you now relax a lot but rarely share enjoyable activities together, it is because you are not *creating* the energy for it. This means shifting some of your energy back towards your partnership.

Make your relationship and the energy you can bring to it a priority. Then define what you want your lifestyle together to look like. Set a plan and be committed to supporting each other in following through. Then call up the energy when it seems like you're slumping, get creative, and enroll your partner in being alive with you! You'll see how easy it is to move towards keeping your relationship interesting and having more balance in your life.

When you find that you are low on energy and it's becoming a regular occurrence, challenge yourself to reclaim some of your youthful enthusiasm. The inspiration must come from within. You will be a lot more fun if you can simply shake off the *habit* of being low on energy. Be conscious about saving, redirecting, or creating energy for your partnership. Do this regularly, and you and your partner will both benefit immensely.

Attitude

Your whole experience of life will be determined by your attitude.

Many people go through life with a consistent underlying "attitude" about themselves, other people, and the world in general. Obviously you can't always control the events that occur around and to you. Yet your interpretation of those events and the way the world is has everything to do with whether you see life as basically good, or instead you are a victim of it. Life is neither good nor bad, but neutral. It is your interpretation, your perspective, and your attitude that makes your experience of life seem like heaven or hell.

The following example illustrates how even just one interpretation a person may make in their life can effect their overall feelings about themselves, their worth, and their lovability:

Out of an act of love, I was put up for adoption at birth. I had been lucky. I didn't get one or two parents who couldn't afford a child, and/or weren't interested in being parents. I was fortunate to have parents who wanted me enough to go through the expense, time waiting, and effort, just to have a child. Yet I could have easily taken on the attitude that I was abandoned and life was unfair.

Many of your feelings about your partner and your relationship are interpretations shaped by your underlying attitude. This attitude is the result of your life experiences, including those with your family, friends, past relationships, jobs, travel, and schooling.

Interpretations usually become more than just "a possibility." Unchallenged, they can begin to appear factual - and the undisputed absolute truth. Some of your beliefs and attitudes about yourself, your partner, your relationship, and even life as a whole can be challenged and altered, opening the door for break-through changes in your life.

People can learn to re-write their mental scripts and become rejuvenated and more alive. They can become more open, more patient, more appreciative, more in love, simply by challenging some of their long held beliefs and maintaining a better attitude.

We can't control how other people such as our children, friends, co-workers, or our partner interprets situations in life - but we can challenge them to re-examine and reconsider their interpretations. Most importantly, we need to challenge *ourselves*.

> *"Reality is something you rise above."*
> *Liza Minnelli*

What we decide is true is not always so. For example, if you believe your partner will never be a more passionate lover, you could create a self-fulfilling prophecy. Or you could challenge your belief and look for ways to infuse more energy and enthusiasm in your sex life together. Your partner could interpret your desire to go on a vacation alone as a sign that you're no longer in love with them. By reconsidering their interpretation, your partner might see how some quiet time alone could benefit you and they may be no longer convinced you are tired of being with them.

You may need to also occasionally challenge your interpretations of your partner's comments or actions. Here is such an example:

Mary's husband, Marc, gave her a membership to an athletic club for her birthday. Mary had not asked for such a gift, and thus interpreted it as a sign that he thought she needed to lose weight. Admittedly, Mary had been self-conscious about her weight. After receiving Marc's gift, she decided that her "inconsiderate" husband didn't find her attractive any longer, and his gift was an insult. She believed he didn't respect her because she had put on a few pounds. Yet the only true "fact" was that he had given her a membership. What it meant was not quite so simple, so black and white.

Marc is very practical, and believed giving Mary more clothes or jewelry - something he thought she didn't really need, wouldn't have been as good of a gift as an athletic club membership. Marc probably should have asked her what she wanted, but he preferred the element of surprise. He wanted to give her something she would use, and something he thought she would benefit from for a long time. He had heard her talking about joining a club a few months earlier, and truly meant to convey no viciousness or lack of respect. He wasn't dissatisfied with her body. Instead he simply thought he was being nice.

It could be argued that Marc's money could have been more wisely or safely spent. On the other hand, people make mistakes, and accidentally hurt or anger their partners. It is in situations such as this that we must be careful with our interpretations and assumptions and challenge ourselves when we notice our attitude is far from loving.

Consider wearing yellow-tinted sunglasses. Everything has a yellow tint. The grass is greener, the sky more blue. Is the sky actually more blue, the grass really greener? Your attitudes are similar to tinted sunglasses. Through your "attitude" you look at the world and decide what everything means.

Our attitude colors our interpretations, and our interpretations change or reinforce our attitudes.

Take for example a "bored" person. Being bored is a state of mind. There may be times when there isn't anything exciting going on or isn't anything that you feel like doing. But the absence of stimulation does not mean 100% guaranteed boredom. Some people would enjoy this quiet time, while others mope and complain about being bored. Your experience is determined by your attitude.

This is not a pie-in-the-sky philosophy of "maintain a positive attitude in life and everything will be blissful and perfect." There will be times when you are sad, hurt, angered, or a little blue. That's simply the result of being human.

We all experience a wide range of natural emotions. Yet there are times where a person needs to turn around their negative attitude when they catch themselves slipping into an unhappy downward spiral.

When hearing yourself complaining or finding fault in your partner or others around you, make a conscious effort to re-direct your energy, finding it within yourself to create a new attitude. There's always a multitude of ways any situation can be interpreted.

We occasionally need to get back to the attitude
that interprets life as a gift, as something that is good,
and that what we want is possible.

Attitude will make all of the difference in your interpretation and experience of life - and especially of your partner, including what they may have said or done, and what it means. Most people never challenge their own interpretations. Let go of being right and instead keep in mind that your way of seeing things is simply *your* interpretation. When you express yourself to your partner and others with this in mind, the easier it will also be for them to listen to you.

Your attitude can drag you down slowly into the quicksand of misery, disappointment, and frustration, or instead serve as a trampoline, helping you bounce back quickly. Your attitude is a choice. By being more aware of your "attitude" and the power that it has in coloring your interpretations, the better you can get at choosing your attitude. This dramatically improves your chances of enjoying your life & your partner.

If You Could Go Back

Pretend that for a fee you could pick a time of your life, anytime that you want, and re-experience it. For one day you'd be there, the same age you had been, in the same place, with the same people.

Imagine actually feeling the same feelings, seeing the same scenes around you as you had, eating the exact same meals. The music you would be listening to would even be the same.

The power of such an experience would be incredible. Can you remember the days when you first met your current partner? Wasn't life grand?! Weren't you energized about life and on top of the world, excited when your lover called, and willing to change your schedule at all costs to make time for each other?

Chances are you had all kinds of ideas of things you wanted to do together. You talked on the phone for reasons other than to just take care of the basic business at hand. You both had a lot to talk about, and asked a lot of questions. You were proud of your partner and talked about them, with positive adjectives and descriptions, to your friends on a regular basis. You were both playful and smiled a lot. Your enthusiasm in life increased dramatically.

Do you remember being incredibly forgiving, patient, and understanding, often going out of your way to do something extra or special for your new partner? You laughed, held hands, and maybe even unlocked the car door for each other. When there was one bite of the decadent chocolate dessert left, you gave it to them. *If you could just touch that time again, even for a few hours.* Some people discount the past, as if it was less significant than here and now. This isn't to say you should live in the past. But the past was as real and valuable in the whole scope of your life as the present.

If you have a happy picture of the two of you when you met,
enlarge it and hang it in your home.
Use it as reminder of where you started from,
and what is still possible for you to have together.

Your life is yours to enjoy or let slip away. Every hour and every day passed is irretrievable. Listen to the way you talk to your partner. Does it sound the same as it did when you first met and were excited, intrigued, and interested? Or does your voice often reflect disapproval, frustration, impatience, or resentment?

Catch yourself being ornery, sarcastic, or critical, and ask yourself,
"How would I have said that if this was our first date?"
Put some of that compassion, understanding, sweetness,
and warmth back into your voice.

Challenge yourself to put the same level of understanding, energy, and compassion into your relationship as you had at the beginning. Use the sweet memories of the past to remind you of who and what you have. Life may seem irreversibly different than in those first days together. Many miles have been put on together. You have seen each other at your best and worst. Focus on the good you *had* and *have* now.

Design the kind of life that you'll be grateful for and proud to look back at someday. You know you can't freeze time and life will never stay the same. Even so, you *can* keep your relationship interesting and fun. Close your eyes and hold your partner, and think back to when you first met. Remember what it was about your partner that you fell in love with. Think of some of your favorite memories together. Think about the things you had always wanted to do, but never did, and make plans to do some of them.

The nostalgia of your past together can be like an old covered bridge, bringing you back to the love and enthusiasm that existed and is still possible between you and your partner. By remembering those early days occasionally, you can return to being more of the wonderful, loving person you once were.

~

"Argue for your limitations,
and sure enough,
they're yours."
Richard Bach

Chapter 5

Hunters And Gatherers
The tug of war between the genders

~

Many of the conflicts that couples face are related to the individual perspectives, attitudes, and behaviors of each partner. These differences can be the result of many factors, such as birth order, the area in which one was raised, the financial and social status of one's family, the decade in which they were born, or even how many parents a person had. Yet many of the most common differences are shaped by our gender as well as our unique personality style. In this chapter we will begin looking at some of the gender differences and how they can effect a couple's relationship. Later in the book we also explore the element of personality differences.

A Note From The Author

Imagine that a sociologist was studying the behavior of men in different parts of the country who had just purchased a newspaper. After watching 1000 men, they counted 900 who opened their paper and went directly to the sports section. It would be fair for this sociologist to draw some conclusions, thus creating generalities, such as most men first look at the sports section before the rest of the newspaper. While not *every* man does so, most do.

As I talk about any group throughout this book, especially in the sensitive area of gender, please remember that I refer to the majority, what *most* men and women do, not all. There are always women who seem to possess some typical "male" characteristics, just as there are also men who possess many of the characteristics typically found in women. Men and women are just too different and unique to be conveniently categorized. Yet there are commonalities that many men and many women share. While you may be the exception to the rule, please keep in mind that I refer to *many* and *most* throughout the book.

Tug Of War

Men and women often believe that their way of living is the "right" way, and when their partner shows up as different, they seek to change them. Men and women often feel their partner is "broken" because they are so different. They mistakenly believe that if they could only get their partner to adopt their own way of interacting with the world, they would both be much happier. Thus the tug of war occurs as men and women try to change each other to become more like themselves.

A woman recently told me that men were not emotional enough. She felt that women had to compensate for their man's lack of emotion, making women overly emotional. She stated that women could be less emotional if men would only become more emotional. This woman was determined to get her man to become more emotional. Is his calm and low-key approach balancing and a benefit, a limitation, or possibly both? Are her beliefs and attempts to change her partner reasonable, or will they simply frustrate both of them and end up being an exercise in futility?

Fortunately neither men nor women are broken, just different. By accepting these differences, we improve the possibility for long-term survival of the relationship with an increased level of mutual respect and appreciation. This is not to suggest that neither partner can grow and change by learning from the opposite gender. Rather, the challenge is knowing what change is reasonable and what we should accept as not only normal but also mutually beneficial.

Some men may be able to tell you all of the different but wonderful things about a woman. Yet when it comes down to a day-to-day life with women, men often wish their partner was more like themselves. They wonder why women have to be so emotional? Why can't they just let go of things? Why can't they solve problems the way men do? Why do women have to talk about everything? In a sense, some men believe that if their partner was more like he was, she would be happier and have a better life. He could love her more, and their problems would vanish!

Women often operate in the same manner. First, they find a male who they think can work with and who shows some signs of hope, and then they set out to tune him up to be who they want their partner to be. Many times these women become frustrated when their efforts don't create the degree of change they had in mind. They ask why their partner can't communicate like their women friends. Why aren't men more emotional? To many women, it seems men's priorities are all wrong!

Maybe you've already overcome these human urges I speak of, but remember the others out there who have also picked up this book and may be still facing this challenge. Understanding that we have this tendency to try to improve others does not change the fact that most of us still haven't mastered *not doing it!* We need to allow our partner to be different and not think of their differences as being limitations or faults. Many will live a whole lifetime & never master this challenge.

We Are Different - Not Better

I'm all for equality. After all, no man or woman, anywhere in the world, should be considered worth less than another. But let's be realistic, men and woman are different. We can not seem to get this through our heads, even though all of the obvious outward signs are there, that we *are* indeed very different creatures.

Certainly much of what makes us different is centuries of conditioning that men should be a certain way and women another. Just as significant is the role our genetics play, since there are many natural differences in our bodies and minds.

As a society we don't need any more is excuses for undesirable behaviors. We are not held captive to our links to the past, whether we're referring to genetics or conditioning.

At this point of our physical, emotional, and intellectual advancement it is quite clear that our modern brains can override many of our instinctual urges and tendencies. As a society and as couples we will benefit from bringing men and women together instead of dividing and separating.

We are not from separate planets but rather from the same origin, and can get along much more easily than many seem to believe. While we may be capable of much more adaptation and change in the future, men and women are still different creatures presently.

The difference between men and women isn't just their sexual organs

For an illustration of how different we really are, consider the following examples from the science journalist Marc McCutcheon's book, "Astonishing Facts About Human's:"

Women are reported to suffer 10 times more headaches than men, and are more prone to acute gastrointestinal problems, arthritis, diabetes, and hypertension than men. Men are especially vulnerable to personality disorders, including drug and alcohol abuse, where women suffer more from anxiety, phobias, & depression. Women are more likely to attempt suicide, yet more men actually succeed at it. Marriage increases the risk of depression for women, & decreases it for men.

Women's longevity is far greater over all than men in the U.S.. During the first year of life, 54 males die for every 46 females. By age 21, there are 68 male deaths for every 32 female deaths. And finally, by age 65, there are 7 surviving men for every 10 women. Women outlive men in nearly every corner of the globe and specifically in the United States by more than 7 years.

Men are more violent by nature than women. In 1987 men committed seven times more homicides and aggravated assaults than women. Men also caused two thirds of all road accidents. Numerous studies have shown that aggressive behavior is closely linked with high testosterone levels. Men have higher levels than women. This level peaks when men are young adults, which is also when they commit the most crimes and get in the most accidents. Yet testosterone decreases in production with men over time, while after menopause it increases for women.

Young adult males average 50% muscle and 16% fat, where females of the same age have 40% muscle and 26% fat. Men's blood quantity is approximately 1.5 gallons, where as women average .875 gallons. Our lung capacity as men is 6.8 quarts, where women's is 4.4 qt.'s (at age 25).

Women usually have more accuracy at identifying odors & tastes, have sharper vision, and are better at hearing high sound frequencies. They also perform left-brained activities better than men, such as processing and learning language. Boys are often slower to speak and are more apt to stutter. Yet these same boys typically excel at right brained activities, gain mobility quicker, and often perform better in mathematics, science, and visual-spatial tasks.

In spite of all of the anatomical, physical differences, somehow both genders seem to overlook the differences and live as if men and women are only different because of the penis, vagina, and breasts. We mistakenly believe that other than their "sexual accessories" our partner should be just like us.

There is certainly some truth to the fact that we are conditioned to be different beginning as a small child, which surely plays a part in the gender gap. Yet some fundamental differences, regardless of their origin, do exist and create problems for couples who refuse to accept the differences and relentlessly try to change their partner.

"The only time a woman
succeeds in changing a man
is when he is a baby."
Natalie Wood

Humble Beginnings

You may have heard it before. We are what we are because of thousands of years of programming from our genetic ancestors. How much is there to it? It's hard to say where to draw the line between what we want to believe and what is in fact "the truth." With a closer look at the average "modern day" man and woman, it seems reasonable to say that at least part of the evolutionary theory may be valid when it comes to trying to understand many of the differences between the genders.

While some may want to believe that we have evolved to the degree that any personality imprinting from our past ancestors is irrelevant, there are some common behaviors that suggest otherwise.

We *have* evolved from the early humans whose way of life was as real to them then as your life is to you today. Men and women were living a life that did not include restaurants, frequent flier miles, minivans, or the Internet.The human existence didn't begin with the creation of anyone who looked or acted anything like Mel Gibson or Cindy Crawford.

It's impossible to comprehend the true length of our lineage, much less anything further back than our grandparents. Yet regardless if we were poofed into existence by God or started as a genetic mutation of some other form of life, we for certain go back to some pretty humble beginnings physically and socially.

Today's environment is certainly different from that of our ancestors. Similar to a fourth generation zoo animal who no longer needs to worry about survival, we still possess the same genetic imprinting as we always have. Now our brains are more in control than they used to be. Just as zoo Zebras no longer need stripes, we no longer need the ability to sneak up on animals for our survival. Still, five hundred years from now, the ancestors of zoo Zebras will still have stripes.

It makes perfect sense that genetically we were originally programmed for certain things to aid in our survival. That we no longer need to rely on many of our basic instincts for survival is irrelevant when one acknowledges that we were given these gifts as a species as was the giraffe, greyhound, and polar bear. What are some of those original genes that we were given to help us survive? Do they still play a role in our daily existence and challenge the genders in their efforts to get along?

Hunters

One of the original gifts that genetic imprinting gave early man was the instinct of fight or flight. The intense adrenaline surge in the face of danger helped man react quickly. It seems that even today men tend to have a shorter fuse than women and can become intensely angry and defensive in a flash. Since men don't always feel comfortable with this intensity when they are around the woman they love, often their brain kicks in the flight response as a safety valve in order to diffuse their anger and emotion.

Back when men spent the majority of their days on the hunt, dressed in either hides of animals or even nothing at all, life was certainly different than now. There were no semi-automatic weapons or four wheel drive trucks. Life was simple, and men were doing what came naturally to them. Men didn't go to seminars to learn how to change, modify, or redirect their lives. Rather, they were great "hunters," whose approach was significantly different from the rest of the animal kingdom.

A modern "hunter" will joyfully tell you the tricks of the trade that help them be successful in their predatory escapades. Here, some basic rules are just as true as they were thousands of years ago. One of the more simple concepts is silence. To be effective in the wilderness, man has to blend in as much as possible. This means being cautious and stealthy. Man's ancestors would spend days on end out on a hunt. Space, open air, and quiet were a way of life. They often didn't return until they'd been successful. When the food was gone, they were off again.

A friend of mine was out hunting recently when he noticed that over an hour had passed since he or the other two men he was with had said a word. Neither of them was the least bit uncomfortable with it. Silence came just as easily to these 3 men as it did a couple thousand years ago to the "hunters" of that time. Doug mentioned this to the other men. They grunted in agreement, and then fell silent again for another hour or so.

While complete silence isn't always necessary out on the hunt, not having the need to talk is a good trait to have come naturally if you must rely on hunting for your meals. It's hard to be stealthy and to blend into the habitats of others in the animal kingdom with a lot of chatter. It could even be said that what was a natural benefit to our early ancestors could be one of our most significant Achilles' Heels as men try to get along with women in today's more cognitive and verbal world.

Women are no longer satisfied with the primitive "hunter" who just brings home some fresh meat - they want someone to talk to and relate with. Men can no longer use the excuse that men just don't talk. While it may not be as easy for some men to open up, it is possible.

There is no genetic floodgate that needs to be opened, just a willingness to try. Yet many women could adjust their expectations of how expressive their partner can and should be. Women can also be more understanding regarding the years of conditioning and the remnants of genetic imprinting that influences their partner, becoming more patient as he stretches to be more verbal.

Doug was going for a two hour drive to the coast to stay at a romantic bed and breakfast with his wife. He was patiently driving and day dreaming, enjoying the drive and peace and quiet. At the same time, his wife Natalie was feeling disappointed. To her, the silence was disturbing. She was hoping they would have been able to catch up and share some interesting conversations along the way, but Doug didn't seem to want to talk. She wondered what was wrong, why he was being so quiet.

Natalie continued thinking, "I wonder if something is bothering him? Maybe I did something to upset him and he just doesn't want to get in a fight. Maybe he's bored with us. Or it could be that he's worried about something at work and doesn't want to worry me about it. I wish he would just open up and talk to me more easily."

In actuality, Doug was thinking about how the fall colors on the trees reminded him of being a child. Yet because this silence doesn't come that naturally to some women, they may think it's odd or something to worry about when their man is quiet. In fact, many times there is nothing to worry about; he's just daydreaming or being quiet. *To be fair, some couples are reversed of the norm, with the man being talkative and the woman more withdrawn.*

Man, while being verbal, are often brief and speaks in short sentences. That can easily frustrate some women, as they want and expect more of an "effort" on their man's part. They enjoy a more verbal approach, and can be disappointed with his lack of interest or ability in communicating.

At the same time, men can become irritated by all of the talking being done by women. As Doug shared with me: "Talk talk talk. Can't women just relax and not always have to talk? When it's been a long day, I just want to come home and have a little peace for an hour or so. But as soon as I open the door, my wife wants to tell me about her day, asks how mine was, and how I felt about it."

Another significant difference between the genders is the need for "space." Keeping in mind that everyone's definition of a balanced relationship is different, here is an example of what a man recently expressed to me regarding his need for space:

Joe said that his relationship was perfectly balanced when his partner was home for four days and then gone on business for three. Four on, three off, four on, three off. Week in and week out. Why? Because he loved being with her for four days, and then he could have his space for a few. By the end of the three days, he would miss her again, and thoroughly enjoy being with her for the next four.

Many women don't have or understand this need for space, and take it personally that their partner likes to be away. Our hunter ancestors were very independent and quite used to being alone. The time by themselves didn't "mean anything" then, and it doesn't always now. The average urban man isn't going off into the woods for days on end, yet it doesn't mean they have no need for some space or solitude.

The busiest male executives may never make the time for any of this quiet personal time or ever learn to enjoy the peacefulness of being alone, and can still lead satisfying lives in spite of it. Some men's work environment gives them this space, such as some construction jobs, farming, accounting, or engineering.

Many men whose jobs don't give them that quiet take up hobbies like reading, computer games, going to the gym, or getting away by going fishing, hunting, or hiking. I'm not implying that women don't enjoy having some space; rather it's just more important to many men. This desire to have time outside of the relationship is natural, and doesn't mean men are seeking it to avoid their partner. Some men feel overloaded with the level of involvement that many women require, and want life to be more simple and basic for a short while. Yet they truly love and appreciate the woman in their lives, and know that too much time by themselves can also be quite boring.

The Gatherers

Even the empowered women of the nineties, embodied by people like Hillary Clinton, Marcia Clark, or Barbara Streisand, are descendants of primitive "gatherers." Women's humble beginnings are also still relevant to some of their traits and characteristics today. Women have no doubt changed dramatically and in many ways from the days of their early ancestors. Yet, women also have inherited some genetic imprinting.

While the men were out hunting, the women stayed close to their shelters with their young ones. They kept busy by gathering berries and other foods. As civilization developed, they began making and wearing clothes. Most of their activities were done in groups, and they spent an enormous amount of time together. As language developed, they had the time and environment for plenty of verbal practice.

A women's natural instinct to care and nurture hasn't changed, and they do it well. The majority of women are genuinely affectionate and warm. Just like the mothers of many in the animal kingdom, they naturally care for their young, which is genetically imprinted for survival of the species. Even though today women often choose to have no children or can use day care and nannies, women will always continue to be born with the nurturing instinct.

Huddled around a stream together cleaning clothes, weaving baskets, or playing with their children, modern women's ancestors learned that "community" and "family" and "togetherness" were good. This way of life came quite naturally to them, and still does today. The women enjoyed being together and found it to be useful. The gatherers teamed together to accomplish tasks, and found comfort and safety in being among others.

Just because many women today work in offices doesn't mean they have changed entirely. Comparisons can be made in regards to the importance women still place on the family being together and doing things as a group. Many women can't understand how some men just don't share their need for as much togetherness or relating to each other by sharing what they are thinking and feeling.

Mary works in a small office of three women. Although they are all very productive, they still find the time to share what is happening in their lives. The women know each other well, including what is happening in their marriages, with their children, and their health. Mary's husband Tom also works with two other men, and has for ten years. Yet other than occasional personal stories, most of what these men talk about is work, sports, and what they did over their weekend.

I remember hearing about a study that had been conducted with small children around the age of five. Little boys and girls were put into separate rooms without any directions and were watched through two-way mirrors. Dolls were put in both rooms, which the girls promptly picked up, dressed, rocked, played with, and talked to. The little boys proceeded to take the dolls apart. Later, both rooms of the children were asked to find a chair and sit and talk to the others in the room. The little girls faced their chairs towards each other and found it easy to talk. The little boys put their chairs side by side and said very little to each other.

This simple study, as well as many others, suggest there is more than just a conditioned difference between the genders. Even if some of our differences are the result of long-term conditioning, is it reasonable to expect an adult to completely erase or override thirty or forty years of conditioning (much less a couple hundred thousand years of the species) in order to reinvent their way of interacting with the world?

It is perfectly normal and healthy for men to be nurturers, just as it is for a woman today to not feel obligated to be "the nurturer." There is much room for overlap in which men can be more like women have been traditionally, and women can be more like men. While we have advanced as a society to accept these changes, some men and women are firmly entrenched in what they know and have been for all of their lives.

Remember, it's easier to change your expectations and your relationship than it is to change your partner. Trying to completely overhaul your partner is a recipe for years of frustration. Complete change is not necessary for happiness, but a little here and there is possible and can be quite helpful.

Many people experience conflicts when they try to change a partner who doesn't want to change. Much of this could be avoided by more acceptance of who your partner *wants to be* as well as adjusting your approach as you try to bring about change, which we'll talk about in greater depth in upcoming chapters.

Because of the differences between the genders, we need to use our minds to keep our attitude in alignment with the spirit of understanding and compromise. Since our society has advanced and our expectations for each other have increased, both genders need to stretch a little now and then. Men and women need to acknowledge their partner's needs as being valid and important. For example, women can be more supportive regarding her partner's need for space, and men can make more efforts to communicate and spend more quality time with the woman in his life.

In the next chapter, we will look more closely at other specific differences between the genders and the challenge they can bring to relationships between men and women.

~

CHAPTER 6

Dancing To A Different Tune
How men and women can bring balance into each other's lives

~

The differences between the genders surface in many daily areas of life. It's quite common that couples will experience conflicts regarding issues such as parenting and the use of discipline, spending money, the use of their time, and household roles and duties. Also, men and women often feel quite differently about how to solve problems, what their priorities should be, and what interests them. If you are in a relationship, many of the differences between the genders in opinion and approach have probably surfaced from time to time. In this chapter we'll look at some of the areas that create most of the friction because of a lack of understanding or acceptance.

Linear & Spontaneous

As discussed in the last chapter, many couples find the area of communication to be one of the more challenging aspects of their relationship. Men are often not very verbal and expressive, where as many women enjoy and excel at sharing their feelings, thoughts, and concerns. Women are often more engaging and skilled at creating rapport with people, and usually more involved and interested in others. This helps women be great managers, teachers, and mothers.

Since communication is the thread that weaves through all of the other aspects of a couple's relationship, it's evident that this difference in approach is important as it can make getting through other problems even more difficult.

Men tend to be very linear in the way they think, solve problems, and communicate with others. "Linear" in this sense means their thinking follows a "logical" path such as following the alphabet, A through Z. When a man begins telling a story, he will almost always draw a complete circle so that the beginning makes sense and is relevant to the ending. When someone begins telling a man something, he often is looking for where the storyteller is going and the "bottom line." When it's apparent to him that there may not be a bottom line or it could take a long time for the speaker to get there, a man will usually become impatient.

If Don is talking about driving to San Francisco, it may make sense to him that the subject will remind him of his cousin who lives there; a very linear connection. However, if his wife Suzanne suddenly changes the subject to designing a new patio in their backyard, Don will immediately wonder where the "link" is. Don thinks there must be a connection between the two subjects, while there very well may not be. Suzanne is not crazy or insane. She is simply more able to think outside of a linear train of thought more easily than Don.

This tendency of men is important when a woman wants to express something to her partner. If her approach begins to appear as if the conversation could be excruciatingly long, a man will often try to cut to the chase and save a lot of time. While this may not be an endearing feature to a woman who enjoys relating to others, and who wants to do so with her partner, it is a relatively common male attribute. Men can learn to become more patient and women can learn to make some of their conversations more concise and clear.

The linear characteristic of men can be both a strength and a weakness. This "ability" helps them stay organized, focused, and striving towards completion. This is a perfect trait to have for the gender that places so much emphasis on accomplishment. The linear approach to life can also be boring at times, and quite limiting when creativity and imagination are needed.

The wide range of clothing options for women is testament to their diversity of their self-expression. Their sometimes idealistic beliefs can be refreshing, uplifting, and balancing to their more realistic and sometimes cynical counterparts. Women tend to be more emotional, abstract, and spontaneous. While these attributes can make shopping a dangerous endeavor from a financial perspective, they are also very special gifts that bring life to a man's methodical world. Many women think in a more random manner than men, which can easily lead to major changes in direction of conversations. Being random is what my wife, Kris, and I call "A woman's prerogative."

Because so many men are "practical," they often neglect to appreciate the value of things that they see as unnecessary.

A man who attended one of our seminars gave one of the worst gifts imaginable to his wife. She wanted a necklace for Christmas, but because it was impractical, he spent the money on a Stairmaster for her. Needless to say, she wasn't happy.

Men are usually quite linear when they try to solve their problems. They first seek to understand and make sense out of their problem as in figuring out a puzzle. Looking for a "rational" and "practical" solution requires the ability to concentrate and focus. Thus many men find it helpful to retreat to a comfortable and peaceful setting without too many distractions so they can think. Where many women like to share this process by talking it through with others, men often like to "figure out" their problems in isolation by doing things like going for a walk, listening to music, building birdhouses, or going for a long drive.

Because they don't usually solve problems with the free-form thinking pattern of women, this concentration isn't always as easy to do for men while in conversation. This process is also relevant when men become stressed or upset, as most men prefer to retreat, calm down, get things into perspective, and then solve the crisis. It is hard for men to think clearly when they are upset and they know it. Because men don't like feeling angry, they want the feeling to go away, and the quickest way for that is to retreat. A more calm state of mind is instrumental in "figuring out" their problem.

Meanwhile the woman in a man's life is needing to talk things through and resolve the situation together as a team. His emotional, verbal, and usually physical departure scares her, leaving her concerned about their strength as a couple and the volatility or remoteness of her partner. His retreat is often mis-interpreted as a gesture of his disgust, rudeness, immaturity, or maybe even insensitivity. Both partners need to work towards more tolerance of each others approach, and strive to compromise and stretch to meet each other's needs.

The non-linear way of life is also helpful at times for women as it can help them switch gears emotionally and mentally more easily. For example, at the end of a work day, it is often hard for many men to "switch off" work mode and be relaxed, playful, or intimate. Women can be more understanding of this male tendency and give them a little time to adjust their mood and focus.

The creative nature of women can also be of great value when solving problems. It's easier for many women to think "outside of the box" and come up with interesting alternatives and solutions to challenges. Men would do well to occasionally give up their independent nature and enlist the free-flowing thinking of their partner when faced with career/ work problems.

As both people accept and understand their partners way of attempting to communicate and resolve problems, they can become less upset by the differences and instead find humor and a more good-natured spirit about the whole situation.

Emotions & Feelings

One of the most common areas for frustration is how we experience, handle, and express emotion. Most women express emotion easily and have a lot of practice doing so. Men on the other hand are thought to rarely express emotion, aside from occasional bursts of anger.

Women usually prefer to share their emotions with other women. They believe that "feelings" are real and worthwhile, and by sharing what they are going through with others they deepen their connection and establish solid, meaningful relationships. Since sharing what's going on inside is often easy and natural for women, they typically believe that it should be the same for men as well. While women tend to share their fears, hurt, sadness, and other feelings more naturally, men tend to express anger and frustration more easily and often.

Yet a woman may see her man watch a sport or political scenario which he really cares about - and she sees a man expressing emotion. Sometimes women mistakenly believe that he should be just as able to express his personal emotions with her, if he really loves her.

While it seems common knowledge that most men just don't naturally and easily express vulnerable or sensitive feelings, some women are sure they can train their partner to be otherwise. It is possible for a man to grow in this area by becoming more comfortable communicating and dealing with conflict, which we will address in upcoming chapters. However, it's important for a woman to not expect him to learn to do so overnight or upon command. Major problems can occur because a woman expects her man to experience the same kind of feelings as she does, and then to share himself with her as she does with him.

Men regularly condition each other to "play by the unwritten rules" of being a man in part by discouraging other men from being too "personal." Men know they have received a stamp of approval by society for expressing frustration and anger, yet other men are often quick to keep them in line if they start getting "too sensitive" with them. Yet their partner wants access to what's going on inside, something he's not used to revealing. Sometimes men have occasionally shared their feelings, only to create upset, hurt, or anger with their partner, which reconfirmed that this was not such a great idea.

Here is how Janet, a woman who came to a *"Keeping Love Alive"* seminar, described her first husband:

"Kevin could tell you in great depth and detail about his family, his business, his health, his vacation, or his childhood. But try to get Kevin to tell you his fears, his frustrations, his insecurities, and his "feelings." There wasn't a vacuum strong enough to suck these things out of him. He seems to have almost no experience ever doing so, and thus makes no real concerted effort to break through his "self-imposed" barrier. When he became angry, he would be very verbal at first. But then Kevin would retreat. Getting him to open up again was like prying open a stubborn clam. Sometimes the only way to get him to come back out was to make him angry again."

It has happened in the history of mankind that men have shared their feelings with others, but most men have a difficult time of it. Thankfully more men are beginning to learn that they can share themselves with others and not lose their masculinity and self-respect.

I've seen men learn to be more able and willing to express their feelings and emotions, and I have seen men temporarily transformed by the experience. Many slip into their old ways again. But movement is occurring for many others, and by utilizing many of the tools of this book the process can be even easier.

In the meantime, women would benefit by being more understanding and patient regarding this phenomenon. Men *can* learn how to open up, and women can learn how to make this easier for them. We'll cover more on how this can be done later.

Another basic difference between the genders is not just what emotion we express, but emotion that we simply feel. Most women feel a wide range of emotions, have higher highs and lower lows, and have more variance from day to day then men. Men on the other hand tend to be more consistent with a smaller range of emotional highs and lows. The advantage is they don't usually get as depressed as some women, and the disadvantage being they don't typically experience the wonderful highs either.

Women often stay with things that upset them longer than men, who usually simply want to move on. After men calm down, they are occasionally willing to just take the heat and admit to being a jerk if they think it will result in the end of the conflict.

In the morning Joan and Sam have an intense argument about their son, Billy. Joan talks to her friends at work about their disagreement, and thinks about it on her way to and back from work. By dinner Joan is ready to talk about their difference of opinion again, while Sam, on the other hand, wants to make up and forget about it. After working all day, Sam is tired and hoping his wife will have moved on.

Sam and Joan are following the typical strategies of their genders. And chances are good that she'll attempt to get him to spend another hour or so talking about it at dinner, and he'll try getting her to adopt his strategy and forget about the conflict. While men can be quite unpleasant when upset, they typically don't like to be in that kind of space. Men are often uncomfortable with feeling strong emotions for a long period of time. It's not that men don't care about their relationship and that's why they don't want to talk. Instead men just want to relax, and if talking will probably lead to conflict, they'd rather not.

The wall we bump into is the mistaken belief that the other gender should feel the way we do and that we can get them to handle their emotions the way we do.

Men also get their egos scraped and bruised, and become depressed, sad, and worried as well. However, it's usually hard to see these feelings and human emotions in a man because of their armor and the belief that they must project a strong image to those around them. Many times when men are upset, worried, or depressed, what is expressed is anger, their most commonly expressed emotion.

Overall though, men tend to have a smaller range of ups and downs, highs and lows. They can be so calm and nonchalant that their "stable" mood irritates the woman in their life, who feels like her man is boring and not very alive. When a man's guiding philosophy happens to be one of achieving a "calm" state of mind, it would be perfectly rational for them to not only attempt to be less angry, but to also not be as excited and passionate. The majority of women I talk to say they love their husband, yet just wish he was more passionate!

Women usually feel more emotions more often and are more at peace with doing so. Some women actually seem to enjoy being upset about something. Many times women "like" to take their time getting over upsets so they can really *feel* it. When they're good and ready, and not a minute before, they'll let go of it and move on.

This may irritate men, whose strategy is to move on without too much baggage. Men need to be more patient with the way women process and deal with their emotions. When mood swings kick in, they need to learn how to back off and let her go through what she needs to. He can't fix it for her, and he certainly doesn't want to imply to her that she's weak and overdoing it because she doesn't handle it all in the way that works for him.

As you look at all of the challenges regarding how different you and your partner are, harmony is not the result of converting the other person to agree with or be just like you.

Priorities

Another basic difference between most men and women are their priorities, which effect the choices they make and lifestyle they lead. A classic example is the man who finds it more important to work than to spend time with his children. While some men are getting better at achieving balance, historically this imbalance has occurred frequently and created many problems.

The challenge of having different priorities is especially true when the top priority of a woman is to be with her man, yet his priority doesn't necessarily include being with her. Consider the following example:

Jack's priority on Sunday is to plant himself on the couch with peanuts and beer and watch 3 football games back-to-back. He feels he deserves this day of relaxation. His wife, Judy, may find that her priority of spending a quality day with the entire family at least once a week is not being met. She can come to resent football, the T.V., and Jack.

Her options are either nagging, saying nothing, or to approach Jack (but not on a Sunday) in a manner that has him feel that she understands and respects his attraction to a day of rest and watching football, and yet she wants compromise because her priorities are important as well. Judy went with her third option, and now the family spends the day together every other Sunday and Jack can relax on "his" Sunday without guilt.

As mentioned, women have historically been more motivated by intimacy, love, and family. Many women place their relationship and their children as their unquestionable, number one priority. Even though men tend to value these same things, often they are more motivated by accomplishment, careers, activities, hobbies, and relaxation.

The man who is always out fishing or the man who works 60-80 hours a week is living proof of a slightly different philosophy and set of priorities in action. Many of the men who spend great amounts of time at work say their priority *IS* their family and they are working to provide for them. The difference being in their definition of what having a "priority of family" means compared to their wife's, whose includes more time and active participation with family members. Men and women often have many different priorities and *different definitions* of the same priorities.

Couples may find other differences of priorities. Some may revolve around areas such as making, saving, and spending money, or the amount of time to one's self or together as a couple or family. Instead of listing every possible difference of priorities between men and women, let's just leave it that what's truly important is not how we can get our partner to change but how we can live together harmoniously despite our different perspectives.

Expectations

Expectations can set the stage for what each partner feels they will have to do (and not do), what their partner will have to be like, what the roles and rules will be, etc. Regardless of gender, it's fair to say we all have *some* expectations.

For most women, getting married is not just an event as is a rock concert or the Super Bowl. Especially for first time newlyweds, getting married marks their evolution into "womanhood" and to becoming an "adult." Yet even women who get re-married often believe getting married will "transform" their relationship into the blissful co-existence that she's always longed for. Beginning as little girls, the romantic dream has been honed, crafted, and designed over many years. Many a little girl has hoped to meet their Prince Charming.

Many women have a very detailed vision of what being married or being in a long-term relationship means and what it will look like, which forms the basis of many expectations. Quite a few men look at marriage in a more simple manner, some even seeing marriage as an occurrence and a self-imposed change of lifestyle. Many would prefer that life didn't change at all, other than the fact they're married.

Tom had been dating Carol for three years. Carol said it was time they became serious and got married. Their relationship had some weak spots and Tom had been quite non-committal. But Carol figured he'd change and their relationship would change if they were to get married. Tom's rational for getting married was he didn't want to lose her, so he agreed.

Do you think their expectations for what a marriage should be and will be were different? Carol had high hopes and a clear picture of what being married would be like - and Tom was going along for the ride because she issued an ultimatum.

What a man expects from a woman or marriage is often quite different than what a woman expects of him. He wants her to be sensitive but also emotionally strong. He expects her to be feminine and beautiful, but doesn't like waiting for her to get ready, and thinks she takes too long. He wants her to be slim and attractive, yet his own protruding belly isn't a big deal.

Many men mistakenly believe their partner should be the one to feed the kids or the pets, and clean up after him because he worked hard that day. Being married, to many men, means that *she is his*, almost like possession or ownership. He has a home, a car, and a wife.

Men often expect a woman to be his friend, companion, to take care of him, and do things he doesn't like to do himself. They expect a woman to meet their expectations of attractiveness while spending very little effort on being in good shape themselves. They want a passionate lover, yet rarely are romantic and spend minimal energy on important things such as foreplay.

A woman's expectations are also usually great. To many of them a relationship and marriage are much more complex and they expect a lot more involvement from their partner. Of course, men usually feel women have *too many* expectations, and women feel some men have the *wrong* expectations.

Some women expect their partner to be like a best friend (like one of her girlfriends.) She wants him to be strong, yet wants him to be sensitive and in touch with his feelings. She expects him to share what he's thinking and feeling with her, but when he does (or tries to) it's often not enough. She expects him to fix things around the house, but doesn't believe in traditional roles.

She expects him to like going shopping and to the herb farm, and gets frustrated when he doesn't want to pick out the new curtain fabric or kids' back-to-school clothes with her. Isn't his home and family important to him? A woman usually wants her man to be more of a lover than a sexual partner. She expects him to be more involved in a "relationship" instead of being buddies.

How each person comes to being married will play a part in shaping their expectations. If a person felt they were overdue to get married and they needed to find a partner quickly, that would alter their expectations. On the other hand, if someone felt they were truly a great catch, their high expectations would reflect that belief. Naturally they would feel they deserved to be treated as though they were valuable. Consider Sue & Jerry's story:

> Sue was a very attractive woman. Men couldn't seem to keep their eyes off her, and Jerry knew it. Jerry loved Sue, but wasn't sure she'd stick around with all of the attention she always got. So he took the freeway to the altar to try to "lock up the deal" and make her "his."

Jerry's expectations for marriage were that once they were married, he could relax and know that his "wife" was now his and she wouldn't stray. He thought the contract of marriage would guarantee that. In reality, if Jerry didn't continue to be the partner she needed and wanted, the piece of paper wouldn't be enough to keep her around.

Sue's expectations were that Jerry would "step up" his involvement in the relationship because he wanted to be married, and that's what she would expect from a husband, while Jerry figured once he assured Sue he loved her by marrying her he could be *less* involved.

People often ask, "Well, what do I do about all of this?" The "solution" is simple and clear.

> *By understanding and accepting your differences,*
> *you can choose how to interpret & react to them.*
> *By changing what these differences mean,*
> *it changes and alters the way you relate to each other.*

I doubt the category of "expectations" will disappear as a source of major differences between the genders in my lifetime. The most important thing to remember here is that these differences are all quite common, normal, and yet may lead to many of the frustrations that we experience in relationships. They won't just go away.

We can benefit by changing how we look at these differences when they show up so we'll be less upset by them. We need how to learn how to ask for compromise without asking our partner to become a carbon copy of our own gender. We can increase our appreciation of the differences in order to see value instead of limitations. By understanding the differences we set the stage for this occur.

~

"I never realized until lately that women
were supposed to be the inferior sex."
Katharine Hepburn

"Women's vanity demands that man be more
than a happy husband"
Friedrich Nietzsche

Chapter 7

Vive' La Difference

How your unique personality styles can influence your relationship

~

As mentioned in the last chapter, many relationships don't last because of the inability of one or both people to accept the differences between themselves and their partner. While some differences are gender-based, others may be the result of having different personality styles.

The wide range of personalities in the world makes for some very interesting dynamics between people. Different personalities have different attitudes, perspectives, habits, and quirks. They move to a different song, are inspired or depressed by different things. The subject is complex, yet this chapter simplifies it by introducing you to *"The Color Code,"* by Dr. Taylor Hartman. This introduction into different personality types will not only make the information easy to remember and use, but it will also be especially relevant to your relationship.

As with gender differences, when we see things about our partner that we don't appreciate, agree with, respect, or admire, it can often lead to frustration. Because we are different, we mistakenly believe our partner is "broken" and we must change or alter him/her to be more like ourself. Just as a bridge connects two islands, *The Color Code* can help couples with different personality styles bridge the gap between them.

Understanding what motivates the basic personality types will help you understand yourself as well as help you adapt and work with your partner's personality style. This can change what you interpret and feel about your partner.

When you can easily identify your partner's personality style, it will help you predict how they may act in a variety of situations with amazing accuracy. The interpretation of "he or she's broken" can be replaced with,"Their actions are consistent with their personality type." This gives your partner more permission and space to be an individual, leading to less frustration and energy spent trying to change him/her.

Couples can learn more respect and appreciation by simply increasing their understanding of each other's different personality styles. It makes it much easier to see value in one's partner with this new understanding instead of limitations and perceived "handicaps." This doesn't mean either of you will change your style, but rather that you will have more acceptance of what you each bring to the partnership. The key is to end up feeling better about the differences that show up so that you can live with and interact more effectively with your partner.

The Color Code is a personality profile assessment which is easy to remember and apply. In the next section you will learn about the different personalities. At the end of this chapter you will find Color Code Communication, Inc.'s phone number should you want to learn more about the personalities by ordering their audio tape series or books. The tapes and books also include blank assessments that you and your partner can use to determine your own color and personality type.

Four Basic Personalities

While there are many different personality profile assessment tools available, *The Color Code* has a wide range of applications. For example, you can use it to understand how to be more effective as a parent, as a manager, or in this case, as a partner. What makes *The Color Code* unique is that it focuses on "motive." Motive is what drives a person. A person who is motivated by power may also value intimacy, fun, or peace. Yet they are not *as motivated* to pursue those things as they are to pursue power. On a daily basis, each of the four personalities usually expends the majority of their energy on what is *most* important to them.

This system uses four colors to categorize the different personalities. Most people have a predominant personality type or "color." No one color or personality type is "better" than another, yet they are distinctly different. Once you identify what the primary color of your partner is, it becomes much easier to understand what *motivates* them, helping you live more harmoniously with each other.

When you understand what motivates you, don't be surprised if you begin to laugh at yourself more often as you see yourself following the script of your personality type. You will also develop more patience and learn a greater appreciation and respect for the other personality types, which probably includes your partner.

The four basic colors are red, blue, yellow, and white. Each of the four personality types have a motive that is *most* important to them *most of the time.* "Red's" are motivated by power, "Blue's" by intimacy, "Yellow's" by fun, and "White's" by peace.

Most of us have a primary and a secondary personality type. For example, John Doe may be a Red personality, yet he may also have a good dose of Blue. That means it's important for him to be a leader, but he also loves to interact and be around people. Like everyone, John may appreciate having fun as do Yellows, and enjoy quiet time to himself much like many Whites. Yet for John, the fun and quiet time are less of a priority in his life than the Red & Blue aspects of his personality. Let's look more closely at the four basic personality types.

The Colors
REDS

"Red" personalities are essentially driven by power. These people naturally emerge as leaders in a variety of situations. Reds need to appear knowledgeable and crave approval from others for their intelligence and insight. They want to be admired for being logical and practical. Reds want their own way, and sometimes resist others authority.

Productivity, taking action, and accomplishment are important, as is making good use of their time and resources. Reds like to implement ideas and see them through to the finish. What they value they get done as they are determined and diligent in its pursuit. It's common for many Reds to assess how they feel about themselves by considering what and how much they accomplished each day. Reds often live to scratch things off of their "to do" list. Many Reds are consistently late for meetings and other engagements as they try to squeeze in one more task or errand at the last minute. Reds love doing multiple things simultaneously, such as eating or reading while driving, or doing laundry while cutting the grass.

Whatever stands in the way of their ability to be in control or to be productive can easily irritate a Red, such as a boss, traffic, waiting in lines, or incompetence. Reds like to be in the driver's seat and believe they know most everything. Being bored is not a common experience for Reds because their list of things to do is always growing, and there's always something they could be doing.

When something they want is within their grasp,
Reds will take action to try and attain it,
as long as it is something they truly want or care about.

Red's weaknesses often revolve around their passion for being in charge and getting things done. Reds will step on people's toes or work long hours without being asked, sometimes to their own detriment because they burn out easily or don't make much time to enjoy other aspects of life. At times they may have a difficulty relaxing because of their focused and serious nature. A Red husband or wife is often accused of ignoring his/her partner or spending little time with their family because of the drive to succeed in a career.

Reds can become frustrated when they haven't accomplished what they feel they could or should have, and often set standards for themselves and others that are unreasonable. While Reds can be assertive and direct, at times they are also abrasive and insensitive to others. Reds can also be difficult to be in a relationship with because of their high level of expectations and challenging manner.

As Reds are logical, they can be very impatient with a partner who is more emotional. If problems arise in their relationship, they simply try to make sense out of the situation so they can fix it and move on. Reds can become frustrated by a partner who is unable to get over problems or challenges as quickly.

To be successful in a relationship with a Red, be very patient with their authoritative and driven nature. However, for Reds, respect is critical. To be respected you must assert yourself and hold your ground on important issues. A different personality style can help a Red relax and enjoy life more, but it's important to find appropriate times to do so.

When a Red is being compulsive, be supportive while doing your best to help them occasionally break out of the power or work trance for balance. Express your appreciation of their efforts and all they do for you.

BLUES

People with "Blue" personalities are motivated by intimacy. Their guiding philosophy is to connect with others and build legitimate relationships. To them this is the essence of life. Blues enjoy nurturing, sharing, and helping others, but need to be genuinely thanked and appreciated. They sincerely care about people, and their relationships are a priority. Dependable and loyal, Blues also have a strong moral code and enjoy being "good." Since Blues play by the rules, they can have a hard time accepting others who don't. They have a strong sense of integrity, making them very trustworthy.

Many Blues evaluate the success of their life based upon how many close friends they have, how their relationship is doing, and if they are making a difference in other people's lives. Blues need to connect with others, and are skillful in establishing rapport with people. Blues are verbal, social, and feel the most alive when they are interacting with other people. Blues don't mind sharing their problems or insecurities with others because they value closeness and being understood.

Blues are emotional by nature, enabling them to be very involved, passionate, and loving. They can be good artisans, teachers, or parents because they truly care. Yet a typical weakness of Blues is their reluctance or inability to see beyond the heart. They can develop such a close connection that they inspire loyalty with their clients, students, or children without the need to use fear, but can also be manipulated because of their sensitivity. Blues cannot respect people who lack integrity, and hate to see people or animals mistreated or taken advantage of.

Blue's caring and nurturing manner can lead them into co-dependent situations where they are always trying to rescue and help others. Blues are often taken for granted or advantage of. Many Blues will give, give some more, and continue giving, long after they should have quit doing so when their efforts went unappreciated. Blues who do not receive love and reciprocation from their partner may eventually come to deeply resent it, which can result in a decision to stop caring or even terminate the relationship.

*A Blue's willingness and ability
to communicate is one of his or her's
most significant strengths in a relationship.*

Blue's verbal nature leads them to expect a considerable amount of communication from their partner, and they can be quite frustrated when their partner resists. When a Blue's relationship is on the rocks, they can become very depressed, and may have a hard time thinking about anything else. Many Blues have their share of mood swings to extremes, such as high highs and low lows. Although they are very loving, if mistreated they can be equally punishing and resentful.

To be successful in a relationship with a Blue, regularly make the efforts to express your love and appreciation for them. Honor their sensitivity and caring nature, and give the Blue a lot of space to be social with others. When problems arise, it is important to let the Blue share their feelings, and for their partner to listen and reciprocate. Remember, intimacy is especially important to a Blue!

WHITES

Motivated by peace, the White personality prefers to be calm and avoids confrontation, embarrassment, or "inner turmoil." While Blues need to be good, Whites need to *feel* good. Getting along with others is important, yet it is not always for the purpose of developing intimacy, but more for avoiding discomfort and conflict. They appreciate kindness, and withdraw from abrasive or hostile people. Not nearly as social as Blues, White's are particularly fond of their own company and tend to be the most in their element when alone or in small groups.

Whites often welcome a predictable lifestyle, and tend to be very stable and dependable people. They are independent, have a strong and silent stubbornness, and need to be respected instead of controlled by others. Whites enjoy quiet, and typically don't need or desire much contact with people. They don't get bored as easily as others and can spend hours on activities such as hobbies, fishing, gardening, or reading.

Their calm nature can be balancing and they are rarely

confrontational or demanding. An argument with a White doesn't last long as they either don't get upset, are eager to compromise, or they may back down before a full-scale conflict can develop. As parents, Whites may give in to children's demands too easily just to keep the peace, which is something they may also do with their partner.

A White personality brings
stability and calmness to a partnership.

Many people with a predominately White personality enjoy following directions and independently doing their job rather than being the leader of the pack. Whites are not inclined to take risks or do outrageous things unto others, but can be death defying in personal or physical challenges. Change can also be difficult for a White, as it can translate into being uncomfortable in their surroundings or particular situations.

Whites may resist attending social functions and may want to leave early when they do go along. Since Whites prefer a calm approach to life, they tend to retreat from people who are too loud, too energetic, or too emotional.

Getting a White to tell you what's on their mind or what they're feeling can be extremely challenging, as they are not nearly as verbal and expressive as Blues and certainly not as assertive and direct as Reds. It's not uncommon for a partner to occasionally become frustrated with their apparent lack of emotion or sense of adventure that is common for some White personalities.

To be successful in a relationship with Whites, honor their desire for a peaceful existence and allow them the serenity that being comfortable brings. Give your partner some space to be alone if that's what they want.

Don't demand extensive communication, yet you may need to ask your partner to stretch occasionally in order to have your personal needs met and relationship concerns handled. It's especially important to make it safe for Whites to share thoughts and feelings, and acknowledge and appreciate the efforts they do make in this area.

YELLOW

"Yellow" personalities are motivated by fun, and strive to enjoy life. They are extroverted and playful, and enjoy being on center stage. Friendships and popularity are important to them, and love to be noticed and praised. Yellows are drawn to other fun loving people in their quest to skip through life.

Spontaneity is one of the gifts of a Yellow, and they tend to like to keep life interesting regardless of what everyone thinks they *should* do. Bored easily with routine and predictability, by nature they are adventurous and risk takers. The Yellow's youthful and carefree attitudes are a refreshing ray of sunshine in the serious world of being an adult.

Yellows are similar to Blues in that they are also sensitive and emotional, where as Reds and Whites are more linear, logical, and practical. For a Yellow that can translate into having frequent ups and downs, and caring about what people think of them. They may appear nonchalant, yet it's very important for Yellows to be liked and appreciated, as it is for Blues. But Blues attempt to be liked by doing the right thing and by giving love and nurturing. Yellows are liked by being people who others enjoy having around. The most important thing to a Yellow is to enjoy what they're doing.

To motivate a Yellow, find a way to keep
your life together fun
and interesting.

Never demand that a Yellow take life too seriously or work all of the time. Yellows can be fun to be around, yet frustrating when their diligence and focus is needed for an extended period of time. When a situation isn't enjoyable any longer for Yellows they're often quick to move on. It's easy for Yellows to set aside plans for work when offers of fun come their way. As parents, Yellow's can be overly permissive, although not for the same reasons as Blues or Whites, but instead because they want their children to have fun being children.

Another trait of the Yellow personality can be a lack of desire to handle responsibility. Arguments can result from situations such as not balancing their checkbook or staying organized enough to pay bills on time. Their carefree nature can lead to excessive partying or spending too much time with their friends, sports, or favorite activities instead of with their partner or family. Some Yellows don't like be tied down to commitments such as mortgages, and rarely will worry too much about issues such as retirement.

To be successful in a relationship with a Yellow, try to balance the seriousness of your adult lives with pleasure. Don't let your relationship become "work" on a regular basis. You may need to ask your Yellow to stretch in the area of self-discipline and to stay focused and follow through on projects.

Give gifts that will allow you to have fun and adventure together. Invite the Yellow in your partner to keep the Yellow in yourself alive. Give them the space to pursue activities and friendships within reason that can bring them enjoyment. Be patient with Yellow's sensitivity and emotional side, and be sure to give them plenty of love and affection.

Can A Relationship Work With Partners Who Are The Same Predominant Color?

Partners that share the same primary color or personality style usually understand each other quite well. This mutual understanding can lead to compatibility or just as easily leave the relationship lopsided and without balance. The following is a positive & negative possibility of each color:

P: Two Reds could accomplish quite a bit together. They would probably be very active and stimulate and support each others need to grow, and coach each other into being more effective, productive and efficient.

N: Two Reds struggling for control can be extremely competitive. They may work themselves to the bone and save little time for enjoyment. Their expectations for each other could be too high and they may be argumentative or challenge each other too often.

P: Two Blues' desire to communicate deeply will help them enjoy rich relationships with each other. They would regularly express their relationship concerns as well as their love and support, and would both be very loyal.

N: Two Blues could talk problems out forever, taking them a long time to resolve issues or move past challenges. Their mutual sensitivity might also increase the number of upsets and misunderstandings that could occur between them.

P: Two Whites will rarely have any conflict. From their perspective it could be a match made in heaven as they will have a partner that also enjoys the comfort of staying home and following routines. They would appreciate each other's quietness, independence, and lack of aggressiveness.

N: Two Whites may find communication to be a serious challenge when it comes to resolving problems. Any anger or hurt feelings could easily be stuffed away for years and never dealt with. Besides, who would get the marriage license?!

P: Two Yellows will certainly have a good time together. Their shared passion for enjoying life will probably result in many adventures and a lot of laughter.

N: Two Yellows may rarely get anything done. Chances are they'll never have a retirement fund or own an expensive home, etc. They may also have many ups and downs emotionally together, and if the relationship becomes "too much work," the longevity of their partnership may be seriously challenged.

What Colors Are Complimentary?

Having a partner who is a different "color" doesn't automatically balance your personality. No "perfect" match of personality types exists. We all have potential for providing a positive effect in each others' lives, as well as the potential for irritation and conflict.

Most things in life are best in moderation. Even highly-respected qualities such as enthusiasm or honesty can be overdone. When we look at the area of personality, it is possible to be too Red, too Blue, too White, or too Yellow. Any of these personalities, taken to the extreme, can become not only a problem for the individual, but also make it very difficult to be in a relationship with such a person. You may want your partner's personality to be a positive in your life. Yet it's not always easy to see your partner's color as a positive because of the intensity of their personality or certain actions or behaviors they may have.

Usually people's personalities are not extremely dominated by one color, and are somewhat balanced by their own secondary personality type or color. Yet we all have some limitations which we can change and improve to a degree when we need to or want to.

For this to occur there must be a willingness or a desire to be balanced by your partner. This "open door" is a must, for without it, regardless of which personality your partner is, the differences will be seen as a hindrance and a problem. Dr. Taylor Hartman addresses this in his book *"The Character Code"* and on the six tape series.

When you recognize the value and need for balance, then the possibility improves that your partner who has a different personality type can actually be of value instead of an annoyance. You will begin to invite your partner's comments and efforts at making a contribution to your life.

A balanced and complimentary partnership can also lead to becoming a better person individually. The key to remember is that you will never change your partner's primary personality. Yet through your influence they may stretch past their comfort zones, do things they never would do before, or develop some of the strengths that you inherently have. Attempts to change a partner's color usually result in conflicts between couples. Instead strive to accept each other and compromise more often.

All of the four personality types have their strengths and their limitations. As with the two sides of a coin, *all of us* come with limitations that are the opposite of what makes us special. Understanding and accepting your partner's personality type helps you respect the gifts they naturally have as well as accept and understand the limitations that come along with it.

Give your partner the space, permission, and encouragement to be who he or she is. Instead of ignoring needs because they may not be the same as yours, acknowledge and go out of your way to consciously and intentionally see that their needs are met. By accepting your partner's needs you also adjust your expectations.

You can inspire your partner by understanding what their color is motivated by. Give up trying to "fix them" and instead focus on each other's gifts that bring you together. Laugh at yourselves and see the humor in who you each are.

Understanding the four different personalities can help you immensely in other areas such as your career. It can help you understand what jobs would be best for you, as well as assist you in managing different personalities in the workplace. Learning more about The Color Code can also help you as a parent by clarifying how to value and work with the different personalities that your children may have, as well as to be more aware of your own strengths and limitations. I highly recommend that you consider learning more about this valuable program, which will help you be more effective and successful in whatever endeavors you're undertaking in life.

If you would like further information about The Color Code or The Character Code and would like to purchase the books or tape set and personality profiles, call Color Code Communications Inc. at 801-566-8803. The six tape series is only $50 plus shipping, while the books sell for only $16.95 plus shipping. They do accept checks or Visa/MC over the telephone.

~

Chapter 8

Keeping The Peace
Avoiding a war without enemies

~

In the last few chapters we looked at many of our differences, which often leads to conflicts for couples. There are many reasons why we end up fighting with each other. Understanding what upsets us is part of the equation in reducing conflict. The other part is how we approach situations and resolve issues. It can be said that the more effective a couple is at resolving conflicts the stronger the relationship and the more possibility they have for long-term success together.

The next few chapters will focus on important areas regarding conflicts that are relevant to couples. Conflict is the one thing, more than any other factor, that eventually destroys relationships.

When couples fight, they are truly in a war without enemies. While a person may win a battle, in the long run they are losing the war. The last person you really want to fight with is the person you're sharing your life with, as they are your companion, friend, and lover. Still, skirmishes will happen from time to time, and when they do, it's absolutely essential to look for ways to keep the peace in order to get back to loving each other again.

For a moment Joe felt as if his life was a movie in slow motion. Everything seemed to stand out and was more vivid. As Joe focused on Ellen's thin lips while she spoke to him, the rest of her face disappeared temporarily. The sound was gone too, just her mouth was present. Like the neighbor cutting his grass or a dog barking down the street, he had successfully managed to completely tune-out her words, and the anger she was projecting was going right past him.

The whole world disappeared in that moment; only her angry and incessantly moving lips existed. Joe looked over his shoulder at the cuckoo clock on the wall in his den. Some sound came to attention, but only that of the ticking of the clock. He listened to the slow, methodical tick, tick, tick, tick.

Cool as a cucumber, unruffled by his wife's verbal assault, Joe decided at that moment that his life was passing by. Time was running out, and life was too short for this. He decided that it wasn't worth it. To him, Ellen had become annoying, demanding, and completely unappreciative. Her face was red and you could see the veins in her neck. Whether or not she had good reason to be angry, Joe in that moment decided he was gone, that this wasn't what he had signed up for.

Joe had learned to "check out" over the years. It was the easiest way. He tuned Ellen out, wouldn't get too mad, and tried to ignore her. Once in a while her barbs would break through and really upset him. Many times his lack of emotion and nonchalant remarks resulted in an intensified attack. Their fights never lasted long because Joe wouldn't usually fight back. Joe believed he couldn't win and thus it was a futile venture to try, so he simply avoided conflict with her. Unfortunately they never solved anything either. He didn't like getting angry, and resented when his wife did.

For years they both tolerated this pattern. Joe didn't know what else to do because this was his usual survival technique. Ellen didn't know how to get through to him and so she would intensify her long-since-proven ineffective approach.

While Joe and Ellen have a pattern that prevents much resolution, their approach is similar to more than a few couples when it comes to conflict. There are many other patterns of conflict, such as that of their neighbors, Bill and Jan.

Bill and Jan have the perfect marriage, or so it seems. They never fight, and are always willing to compromise or give in to each other in order to keep the peace. Their friends wish it was so easy for themselves. The truth is, Bill and Jan think that they must avoid conflict at all costs. If and when it happens, they are deeply hurt and concerned about their future together as a couple.

One morning they have a little tiff. Jan goes to work yet can't seem to focus. Her feet are clenched and hands sweaty, and she is intensely frightened that their relationship will end in divorce. But when she returns home she doesn't want to bring up that morning's conflict for fear that the problem will deepen. She avoids the entire issue, as does he.

Bill and Jan don't really know how tired each other is getting of things they've been doing. Bill has found her need for orderliness and cleanliness more and more annoying. He watches her clean and re-clean, and thinks she's becoming a little obsessive, yet holds his tongue. Whenever he does a project around the house, he worries that he didn't do a good enough job for her, although she rarely says so directly.

Jan has become increasingly unhappy and worried about their sex life, or more specifically, the lack of it. Bill climbs in bed, gives her a kiss and hug, and then rolls over. With a deep sigh, he's out like a light. She feels ignored, unattractive, and distant.

If you looked closer, you'd find a variety of land mines scattered throughout their "perfect" and harmonious relationship. But they don't talk about them. They actually go to great lengths to make sure that conflict never occurs.

Most people would agree that arguments are unpleasant and not desirable. However, such conflicts often are the result of hurt or anger that is also unpleasant. By bringing up these issues we can move past them instead of sweeping them under the rug. Besides, once couples get proficient at communication, many times issues can be discussed without resulting in conflict.

The 3 Hinds of Couples

When it comes to conflict, there are at least 3 kinds of relationships. Those that go out of their way, to any length, to avoid conflict. Those that have conflict but settle it without major damage, and reach compromises relatively easily. And last, couples who fight passionately, sometimes with explosive and dangerous blow-ups. While some relationships from all three categories end in divorce, you may be surprised to learn that couples who completely avoid conflict are more likely to divorce because they don't address issues that need to be resolved.

Maybe you know a couple who never fought, who you always thought got along pretty well, who once shocked you with news of their separation. It is such a shock because they probably didn't share their unhappiness with each other much less with you.

In their efforts to not rock the boat, to keep the peace, to leave well-enough alone, some couples abandon what's important to them by ignoring their frustrations, disappointments, and hurts. Instead they build a facade like a Hollywood movie set that sends the message that everything is o.k. when in fact it's all a front. While these relationships may last a long time, they tend to end eventually, in a higher proportion, than the other two kinds of couples. This is not to say that fighting is good, but couples that air their feelings, hurts, concerns, and needs are more likely to see resolution, movement, and change.

It may not always be comfortable or easy.
But couples who speak up and learn to do so
in a way that creates positive results improve their odds.

Couples who bury their anger, hide their sadness, and pretend to be satisfied, can only live the lie so long. They try to rationalize the absence of everything they want, dreamed for, and hoped to have. Yet someday they usually have to face the reality and emptiness of their lives. They realize the love is so far gone they just walk away from it all.

You don't need to try to *create* conflict, you simply don't want to ignore important challenges in order to avoid it. There is also no reason to be afraid of conflict either. Couples don't have to fight to stay in love. When there are problems, if you talk about them in a mature and constructive manner, you can repair the bridges, heal the wounds, and grow together as individuals and as a couple.

Conflict is an important, but dangerous, part of relationships. Couples who learn how to navigate the waters of conflict will probably survive without hitting a submerged iceberg. Couples who avoid important issues, deny upsets, and ignore frustrations very rarely make the adjustments to the undiscussed weak spots in their relationships.

If you are both committed to making your partnership work, you won't be frozen by the fear of conflict and instead will bring up the tough issues and get them out on the table. When you eventually get better at solving challenges together you will rarely fight. Conflict can be an ugly, unpleasant reality. Yet if it occurs without deep anger, it can at least give a couple some clues of issues they need to work on.

Try to communicate and learn how to resolve issues without fighting and getting angry. The following chapters will give you some valuable ideas on how to do this. But whatever you do, don't bury it, hide it, or ignore it.

Creating Your Safety Net

It's been a long day for Laura. She has just finished writing checks for the bills when her husband Jack walks in the door.

"Honey, we have no money. I'm worried about it. We have all of these bills and I have no idea how and when we'll be able to pay them. I hate living like this."

Jack explodes with anger. His voice is sharp and words are piercing. "I'm working hard at my new job, sixty hours a week as a matter of fact, and you dare to criticize me!" Jack yells. His new business venture hasn't been making money for quite a while, and he's quite aware of his lack of success. Jack interprets Laura's comment as a statement that he's not doing enough, and it infuriates him.

Laura is not involved in or attached to this new business of his, and is growing impatient as time passes by. She needs to talk about their situation as a team, as partners, and thought her approach was appropriate. And since she wasn't being vindictive in her words, tones, or voice, she is left in amazement as he erupts in anger.

Within seconds her desire to talk about it melts, as does her love and affection for him at that moment. As he carries on with accusations and is pointing his finger in her face, she emotionally withdraws like a scared kitten that runs behind the couch. Laura is afraid to bring this subject up again. The incident expands her fear of communication to other issues as well.

This potential quicksand could end up swallowing the relationship and connection between them. Because Jack tends to get so upset when she tries to talk with him about sensitive issues, Laura becomes afraid to bring up things that need to be talked about. Without a "safety net" she avoids walking the tightrope of communicating with him.

Jenny and her husband, Peter, were at a weekend seminar of ours once. During a break Peter said "I think we should leave. We don't really need this." Jenny responded by saying that she didn't want to leave, and there were a few things that could be better in their relationship. "Like what!?" Peter said. Jenny responded, "Like our sex life, for one." Peter exploded, saying everything was fine with their sex life, and if she didn't think so, then it was her problem. He was upset, and stormed away.

That's having no safety net. The next time Jenny wants to bring up that topic, or maybe another subject as well, she knows that it may not be very safe to do so. She will surely remember what happened last time.

A safety net is basically an assurance that you have that your partner will try their best to listen and then respond in a mature, loving manner. With this in place, even if one's partner doesn't like everything they hear, the important communication can take place without hesitation and fear.

Jack's brother Howard and his wife Suzy have what looks like an entirely different problem. Unlike Jack, Howard is much more easy going and not so volatile. He rarely gets upset, and is a good listener. However, hurting Suzy's feelings is as easy as getting your hair messed up while riding in a convertible with the top down.

Howard feels uneasy talking with Suzy about most issues. It's as if he's walking around in an unfamiliar house in the middle of the night with the lights off, stubbing his toes on furniture that he didn't know existed, and walking face first into walls that he couldn't see. No matter what he does or says, he hurts her feelings, she becomes upset, cries, pouts, or screams at him. He wishes it wasn't so hard. Yet over the years he has learned to walk on egg shells because Suzy is so sensitive.

One of the most common reasons why couples don't communicate is the lack of safety. The safety of knowing that you can usually say what's on your mind without angering or upsetting your partner. You don't need to worry about hurting their feelings every time you express yourself. You can say what you need without fear of them closing down or exploding as a result.

Of course there are no guarantees. People, given that they are human beings, will sometimes get their feelings hurt. They will occasionally get angry. But overall safety is something that is generally present, or isn't.

Take a look at a couple in a restaurant
who seem to have nothing to say to each other.
Chances are there aren't too many safe subjects for them.

Laura is afraid of angering Jack, and so she refrains from bringing up important issues. They don't communicate because it isn't safe to. Howard wants to avoid upsetting Suzy, and in order to not hurt her feelings, he consciously decides they're better off if he says nothing. To an outsider, it is obvious there is no safety and no communication. Land mines are being installed throughout their relationship.

Occasionally we become upset by what our partners have to say. We don't always have to like it, believe they're right, or even understand it. But when we react in a volatile manner, it scares them, and makes them more afraid to bring up things that really do need to be talked about.

Many men have tried sharing what's on their mind with their current or past partners, and have found they get themselves in trouble, or they opened up a can of worms that they would rather not open. Women often say their partner doesn't know how to communicate. Yet when I'm alone with the men they are talking about, often they can communicate without a problem. This is true in part because I'm not their partner, and I'm not going to become upset at what they have to say.

It Takes Two To Make The Safety Net Work

Suzy asks Howard if she looks fat in a certain outfit. He thinks so, and says so. Without a significant amount of safety, this would be a very big mistake on his part. Howard looks at it from the standpoint of, "If Suzy asks me how I feel, I should be *entirely* open and honest. If she asks how I feel about our relationship, I should simply tell her."

Unfortunately, this idealistic approach sounds good in theory, but is not always the best in practice. A little elegance, a little finesse, and some thoughtfulness can shape our communications so that we can be honest but not blunt and hurtful.

We can take some responsibility for communicating in such a manner as to make it as easier for our partner to hear us without getting defensive or upset.

With some skill in this area, we can help our partner continue to make it safe for us. It's unfair to place the entire burden of "safety" upon the listener.

Both people can do something about this. We'll look at this subject in more depth in following chapters. For now, remember that it helps to be careful about framing questions or comments in such a manner as to reduce the possibility of pushing your partner's buttons. Consider this example from Paul and Amber's relationship.

Amber is feeling taken for granted and says "I think you don't appreciate how much I do for you and I'm tired of it." Obviously this is a subject that needs to be talked about, but with this approach defensiveness is likely to follow. Instead Amber would be better off by saying, in a loving manner, "Sometimes I feel like you take me for granted. I can understand how that can happen from time to time. I'm sure you don't intend to do this, but I do need to feel more appreciated."

Removing any implied malicious intent helps soften the subject and is usually the truth anyway. But even the most well thought out statements can set off some people like Paul, who is an explosion waiting to happen. Paul really needs to learn how to make it safe for Amber to talk with him. Amber needs to be able to express the following to Paul:

"If you want us to be able to talk to each other, I need you to try to not get so upset or defensive when I say something. If I hurt your feelings, tell me so, and I'll apologize. But when you start screaming and yelling and slamming doors, I become afraid of you, and want to avoid talking with you about other important things. If I say something that leads to you feeling angry, tell me so. But try not to freak out and get so upset. I need to be able to talk with you."

Unfortunately not everyone's partner will understand or buy into the idea of making it safe. Even so, do your best to install a safety net to make open communication possible in your relationship.

If you consistently criticize your partner's comments, argue that he or she is ignorant, and/or get upset about what is said, step back and remain calm and neutral more often. This is possible when you choose to be more open to different perspectives and more receptive to new ideas and comments. Ask for your partner's opinions, and why they feel like they do, instead of insisting on proving them wrong.

Occasionally, you or your partner will slip and react instinctively. Give each other a break; you're not perfect. But you both can strive to improve by making it more safe for your partner to tell you what's on his or her mind. If you are sincerely interested in knowing what they are thinking and feeling, then safety is critical in providing the space for this to occur. Remember, your partner is not your enemy, and people tend to listen to those who listen to them.

~

CHAPTER 9

Living In A Glass House
Surviving the passionate conflicts

~

A great many relationships do not regularly have major conflicts. Yet occasionally a minor disagreement or argument can get out of hand and the intensity suddenly increases, putting the couple in a very dangerous and volatile situation. While it's easy to suggest that both partners remain calm, in the heat of the moment this advice just isn't very realistic. Knowing that it doesn't make sense to hurt each other is one thing, but not doing so is clearly another. Finding the strength and sensibility to pull out of the downward spiral that a couple can find themselves is not always easy, but it is possible.

It's been a long day for Jean, taking care of their new baby and their 4 year-old son, Jason, all day. She needs a little peace and quiet, and some time to herself. It's time to feed the baby who has been screaming for the past 10 minutes. Jason hasn't been listening to her, and moments earlier he spilled his orange juice on the carpet.

Chris has been driving in stop-and-go traffic for over an hour. His boss had been demanding all day and had vehemently criticized the proposal he had worked so hard on. Chris replayed the frustrating incident over and over in his head on the way home. He was growing increasingly angry at his boss and he regretted not having defended himself and his proposal better.

Chris feels exhausted as he reaches the driveway. Within seconds of opening the door, instead of receiving a warm welcome, he hears the baby screaming at full volume. He takes a deep breath, sets his briefcase down, and walks into the kitchen.

Both Chris and Jean are tired and frustrated. Jean, while she's on her hands and knees cleaning up the spilled juice, asks Chris to *PLEASE* feed the baby. Her tone implies that it's about time he got home and starts helping. Chris clenches his teeth unknowingly while getting a jar of baby food. "You look tired," he says to his wife, thinking he's being sympathetic.

Jean takes his comment the wrong way, and assumes he's saying she looks like she slept in the car for a few days. Without knowing it, gasoline was just doused on the smoldering coals, and combustion is about to occur. Jean, now at wits end, goes over the edge. The silence is shattered with her reply, "If you didn't go off to your "cushy" office job you'd look like this too after a day with the kids."

The line was crossed, and the battle begins. To Chris, Jean's comment was uncalled for. He works hard, and resents the implication that his job is "cushy." In his angry state, he retaliates with a quick and immature comment, "If you were *smart enough* to have a "cushy job" we could hire someone to watch the kids." The yelling and volume increases while the listening ceases. Both are accusing, defending, attacking, and counter-attacking. Negative adjectives are exchanged as both kids begin crying, and the rage is climaxing.

Jean slams the cabinet door. Chris, who is too angry at this point, pounds his fist on the countertop, standing only a few inches from her. They are both screaming at each other, directly in each others face. In the middle of this exchange of character denouncements, Jean realizes that the situation is getting way out of hand, and someone needs to pull the plug so they can regain their sanity.

This turbulence is good cause for concern, as it is too heated and very, very dangerous. To the uninvolved observer, it easy to understand how it all started. But regardless of the underlying story and the reasons for their emotional and mental state, this couple is unintentionally playing with explosives. Understanding why they are tired, upset, and frustrated does not rationalize and justify their method of dealing with the situation effectively.

If you think passionate relationships must involve passionate fighting as well as passionate intimacy, I challenge you to question this belief. A relationship riddled with conflict can work, but the odds aren't good in the long run. Serious damage to the bridge between two partners can occur in a heated confrontation.

If you only have an occasional argument or fight, it is possible to not only survive the situation but grow from the experience as well. However, in order to see this occur, it's important to not let the conflict get out of control as Jean and Chris did. Just as important, both partners must take the initiative afterwards to repair the damage and heal the wounds quickly.

Sometimes a dose of conflict can be like a bucket of cold water, waking two people out of a trance.

Conflicts can make such a dramatic statement that needed change may sometimes occur after the dust settles. Yet there is always a result, always a consequence to our actions. Intensity can be what it takes for our partner to really hear us when we are hurt or badly in need of change. However, that same intensity can quickly get out of control and begin to disintegrate a relationship as if two people were never even lovers.

Sure, conflicts can be useful as they can lead to constructive change. But remember, conflicts are like playing with fire and can be incredibly destructive. They can overshadow all the sweet moments, all the kindness, all of the love two people have shared. Too many conflicts can squeeze the life out of your connection, Loving partners can become two strangers in the same house left with nothing to say to each other.

When a relationship is new, couples are usually more forgiving and much more patient. They make more allowances & are more willing to compromise. New couples are usually able to let go of those initial fights, even if they're full of fervor and intensity - and see past them. We rationalize the conflict by acknowledging that no-one ever promised us relationships would be easy, and loving this person will take some work. Over time most people find it impossible to keep rationalizing anger directed their way. There is a point where it can really begin to hurt and get to you. The frustration adds up. Sure, you might get past it, and find yourselves laughing about it later, or making passionate love once you have "made up." But someday those swords may cut so deeply that you will no longer have the desire or ability to heal the wound.

Many couples exist in the world of conflict so long that not only does their relationship end, but their friendship is destroyed as well. As passionately as they once may have loved, some go out of their way to either hurt or stay entirely clear of their partner. It's a sad reality that could be avoided by learning how to throw water on the fires and by handling the upsets in a more sensible manner.

It is possible to not agree and yet still feel and show respect for your partner. Part of becoming a "mature" adult is learning to get angry less often, to be less angry when you do become upset, and to get over it more quickly.

The combination of two people can be lethal. A person can bring something out in you that you didn't even know existed, and vice versa. If you are used to fighting, you might want try to seeing what life could be like without the anger, disagreements, and frustration. Passion can be great, but fire is a dangerous element. If you are pursuing a relationship with a lot of fire, walk in forewarned, with your head up and eyes open. *Know that you do not have to fight to love.*

Obviously people come with different sets of beliefs, emotions, and motivations. Occasional arguments will happen, and you may hurt each other, intentionally or accidentally. Conflicts aren't "wrong," but don't need to become a regular part of your daily life either. You can get past these occurrences. You can heal these wounds, especially if you don't wait until an infection has taken hold.

Communicate as best you can how you feel and what you think needs to change. Make it safe for your partner to express themself, and respect and acknowledge each other's perspectives and feelings. There may be times when you need to take a firm stand, yet would still do well to sincerely apologize for your inappropriate approach and/or how you treated your partner.

Chris eventually said to Jean, "Honey, I'm sorry I said you weren't smart enough to have a good job. I didn't mean that. I was angry because I felt you were accusing me of not doing enough to help, and I feel I go above and beyond. I understand you work very hard while I'm gone and were probably just tired and in need of a break when I got home. I'm sure you didn't mean to suggest I was being negligent. I do need to know that you feel I'm doing my part. Still, there's no excuse for my yelling and screaming and being disrespectful. I lost my temper and my cool, and I'm truly sorry."

You *can* learn how to express yourself in order to get the results you want without inducing conflict. You can learn how to get less angry, less often, and past it quicker. There's no magic formula or technique to follow that will make this easy every time. It does take a conscious and determined effort to remain calm when you notice yourself becoming upset, and the courage to take the initiative to de-escalate the situation if and when it begins to get out of hand.

Let The Fire Go Out

Assume for a moment that you and your partner are in the middle of a heated fight. Your attempt to resolve the issue backfired, and your line of reasoning instead ignited the flames. Now extreme caution must be used. Let the fire burn down, don't throw anything else on it. If it is smoldering, don't fan it back to life. Let it go completely out - and then deal with it.

Too many people don't have the sense or know when to leave the situation alone, when to initiate a break from the intensity of the moment. This is especially important if you or your partner becomes enraged. Express that you think it would be a good idea if you both took a break. Promise to come back later to continue to the conversation when you're more calm, and then promptly leave.

Don't just stomp away, or chances are your partner will follow, angered by your sudden departure and apparent avoidance. If you have the ability, mention when you think you may return. While you don't need *permission* to leave, common sense says to leave in as mature of a manner as possible. Resist the temptation to throw a verbal dagger or slam the door to be dramatic. Too many people try to get one more shot in before they leave. Just say you *must* leave, that you don't want to escalate anything, and *you will be back.*

Then get out, relax, and breathe. People have different methods for calming down, such as going for a walk in the woods, exercising, or talking with friends on the phone. Regardless of what approach you use to get into a different space, the key is to know when it's in your mutual best interest to separate yourself from the situation.

Even though every cell in your body may be intent on convincing your partner that you're right and "winning," remember that is not what is most important. Instead, working out the conflict with your partner is what really needs to be on the agenda. Unfortunately, sometimes an invisible force grips us when our adrenaline begins to pump, and our clarity of mind seems to evaporate instantaneously. Most anger management techniques become relatively ineffective and the last thing on our mind at this point. The simple act of temporarily leaving the situation may be exactly what you both need.

Because conflict can get out of control, it is important that you don't burn the house down when conflict happens. You can't *ever* take words or actions back, regardless of how much you apologize. I would bet there are a few phrases that a parent, teacher, coach, friend, or lover has said to you in the past that you'll never forget. In the heat of these fights, many times a dagger is thrown that can never be taken back and will also never be forgotten.

We are emotional beings, and many times we get carried away when the fight-or-flight instinct kicks in. Yet the desire to win, to be right, and to say what you feel compelled to say is only a temporary. In a more calm state of mind your ability to be fair, reasonable, and to compromise can return. When you know there is no easy resolution in sight, see to it that temporary time and space gets in between you and your partner. Otherwise what you might end up with is a permanent distance instead.

Remember, if you didn't care about your partner and your relationship, didn't want things to be different or to be better, then you wouldn't care about what they said or did. Your anger comes out of your desire to have it work and your frustration that at the moment what you have is not what you want. If you are that angry - then you probably care quite a bit. So get out, take a breather, and come back when you've regained your sanity and perspective.

Time Doesn't Heal All Wounds

One night my wife got mad and left the house without the usual hug and kiss. "What just happened" I asked myself? My next thoughts were, "Once in a while she sure is sensitive! I know she'll get over it eventually. But, I guess she was right. I was impatient with her. I suppose I did sound a little arrogant. What I was trying to explain to her seemed simple enough. But just because it was obvious to me doesn't mean it has to be for her. I'll apologize when she gets back. I was being a jerk. I think I'll go do something for a while so I'm not here when she gets back. The space will probably do us good."

When Kris first became upset, what do you think I did? I reacted defensively and tried rationalizing my actions. What effect do you think my responses had on her? It extended the duration and depth of her frustration. And what do you think *began* healing the wound? Time? Space? Love? It was neither of these, although they helped. Indeed what was needed was a simple but sincere and heart-felt apology! It wasn't *not seeing each other* that started the process of healing. It may have helped both of us regain our wits and perspective, but the words still needed to be spoken. Acknowledging your error and mistake is a great first step that so many are reluctant to take.

Imagine a bridge survives an earthquake but suffers some minor and hard to spot damage. Years go by and everyone just assumes the bridge is strong and safe. Then one day, during a blustery, windy day it begins to sway. Weakened from its long since forgotten damages, it collapses while you're crossing on it. Our relationships are really very similar to this hypothetical bridge. Many times we just want to move on and forget the conflict we just had with our partner. Why get into it again? Why bring it up? If you don't, the seemingly tiny fractures add to the other tiny fractures, slowly but surely weakening our bridge. The bridge will eventually collapse and we'll be looking across the vast emptiness, seeing our partner on the other side of this chasm, and no longer know how to reach them.

Eventually discussing the situation that brought on the conflict is always necessary. At least one of the two of you may be hesitant to open this can of worms again. *But it must be done.* Just wait until the smoldering fire is extinguished and you're both quite calm and sane again.

Men typically understand the part about leaving. After calming down, they often return ready to give it up and get past it. Usually they have decided the whole thing was no big deal, and some will even accept full responsibility for being in the wrong. They may come back, take the blame, say they're sorry, and try to avoid talking about the issue again because they don't want it to start all over again. If this happens, beware, you are stopping short of the finish line.

While not always the case, some men are willing to take the blame, even when they don't really feel they were wrong or acted inappropriately, just so their partner will drop the issue. While it may be hard to know if your partner is sincere, I strongly suggest that you still talk about the issue and the conflict that ensued again. You do not want subjects to be off limits and avoided in the future out of fear of possible conflict. The only way subjects can remain safe is by talking about them again. This is made more possible by the apologies and having a reasonable conversation about how you handled the situation as a couple.

Often a woman still needs or wants to talk about what happened, even if her partner is ready to accept the responsibility or admit to being at fault. When this is the case, *she doesn't just want to be right,* she wants to reconnect and relate to her partner, and needs to talk it through. She wants to know they understand each other, not just that he's sorry.

Men may wish their partner would just let it go of the issue. This is simply the *process* many women need before they can emotionally move on. Becoming calm often just isn't quite enough for most women. While this may not be a need that the majority of men may have, it is often essential for many women in order to re-establish intimacy.

Sometimes one partner refuses to apologize because they believe they were and always will be right. So why apologize, why take the responsibility? Chances are it is at those times a person is probably over-looking how something could have been done or said differently. Regardless of how perfect the rationalization appears, the situation probably could have been handled with more maturity, respect, and appreciation for his/her partner's perspective. In the recognition of this, even when you feel in your heart that you're right and there's no need to back down or apologize, cease your pointless attempt at being right. It only digs the hole deeper.

Arguing further or trying to convince your partner of your position won't get you what you really want, which is to be enjoying your lives together. Remember, this is your friend, your lover, and your partner for life. If you lived in a glass house, you wouldn't want to be throwing rocks. Likewise, you don't really want to hurt the most important person in your life.

All of us are occasionally impatient, push our partner's buttons, or are challenging to live with. We may step over the line, go too far, or take our partner for granted. Regardless of your gender, age, or good intentions, part of being human means to error occasionally.

Both parties must let go of anger and conflict and move on.
This includes talking about issues like reasonable and mature adults.
Then we must get on with life.

When feeling angry or hurt, you will benefit by learning to accept and forgive the little mistakes. When your partner genuinely takes some of the responsibility, give him/her a break. All of us are only human, and will occasionally screw up. Don't expect 100% perfection. Your partner's imperfections will show up over time.

If you are loved and treated with respect and appreciation, *forgive them.* If you don't, and instead hold onto the hurt you feel for sympathy, ammunition, or for the simple fact that you don't know how to let go of it, then you'll both pay the price. This eats away at your enjoyment of the experience of living, and extends the length of time that you are both unhappy as well.

So the next time you have a spat, you ruffle each other's feathers, one of you steps over the line, goes too far, pushes the others buttons, steps on toes, rubs their partner the wrong way, pours salt in the wound, or sticks the knife in and turns it - try your best to handle the situation in a manner you can be proud of later. Don't battle it out. Instead, take a breather, get your act back together, and regain a more calm perspective.

Return to talk about it, with civility and a genuine sense of mutual respect. Seek understanding instead of consensus. Look for ways to handle the situation differently next time. *And then move on.* Hug each other. Hold one another tightly and don't talk for a few moments. Close your eyes and remember when you first met. Reconnect with each other, and begin moving on emotionally together!

~

"Inner peace can be reached only when we practice forgiveness.
Forgiveness is the letting go of the past, and is therefore the means
for correcting our misperceptions."
Gerald Jampolsky

Chapter 10

Lighten Up A Little

Three ways to travel through life together with a lighter load

~

Going through life with another person is such a long-term endeavor that couples need to make as it easy as possible to be together day in and day out. High-maintenance relationships that have more than their share of problems, upsets, and frustration sometimes begin to seem like drudgery instead of being enjoyable. There is enough seriousness in our adult lives to weigh us down as it is without having to have our relationship be a constant source of work and challenge. There are many things a couple can do to lighten the load, of which my three favorites are as follows:

Sell The Doghouse!

Most everyone knows what it means to be in the "doghouse." Typically this term is used in reference to men, as he's done something to upset or anger the woman in his life, and "She's going to make sure he pays." This could mean a wide a variety of "punishments," and can last for any length of time. To be fair, many times men are also unable to let go of their anger or frustration and use it against their partner for an extensive duration. While this extended period of punishment is not usually referred to as the doghouse, it is essentially an identical situation.

Regardless of who has put whom in the doghouse, the basic reality is that this practice doesn't do either partner any good. One person assumes a parental role, while the other is put in a position similar to being the child. *You do not want to get into the habit of disciplining your partner.* Remember what happens to teen-agers when they are told what to do - rebellion.

The person who "punishes" their partner also pays a price as well. Not only do they end up filling the undesirable role of being a parent to their partner, they also lose because their partner may see their "time in the doghouse" as the price for their actions. Once the penance is paid, they're even. No understandings or agreements may have been made, and the next time around the potential "perpetrator" weighs the penance and a decision is made as to whether what they want to do is worth it. If it is, they again do what upset their partner and again their partner assumes the role of punisher - and the cycle continues.

The doghouse really holds both people prisoners. Imagine for a moment that you locked up a criminal in a cell, and then you had to sit and guard this person everyday, all day long. You would essentially be imprisoned along with your prisoner.

This whole concept of putting someone
in the doghouse should be abandoned, and replaced with
communicating about & resolving issues like two mature adults.

This practice of putting one's partner "in the doghouse" is the result of two people's inability to resolve a problem through communication. A primitive tool for people who don't know what else to do; it ends up punishing both parties and no-one wins. We will cover ways to communicate in the following chapters that can help you reach mutual understandings and provide you with more effective alternatives to this approach.

Howie was warned over and over by his wife Sharon to never go to a strip bar. He knew she felt strongly about it. When his buddies wanted to go to such a place for a bachelor party, he was quite reluctant, and was very concerned that his wife would find out. He knew going would "land him in the doghouse," yet he was intrigued and didn't think anything was really wrong with going to the strip bar.

Unfortunately, Howie did go, and then lied and denied ever going to the bar. When Sharon found out otherwise, the wound deepened. There was no getting out of this situation easily.

Regardless of how you personally feel about strip bars and Howie's actions, I'm sure you would agree that Sharon had ample cause to be upset. What should have been done about the situation? Sharon could've chosen to punish him, but she knew they'd both pay in the long-run this way. She would have to be angry, cold, or somehow distant to the man that she loved. That doesn't translate into a lot of fun for her, and wouldn't give her what she really wanted in the first place.

One option would have been extended verbal assaults or the silent treatment. Sharon could have tried to take away his future nights "with the guys" as if he was grounded. Some people even take out the credit card and go shopping as an attempt to "punish" their partner. Of course none of these approaches gets a couple back on track with appropriate adjustments made to heal the wounds & prevent future problems.

Sharon wanted Howie to show her respect by being honest with her. It was important to her that he understood how much his actions hurt her feelings. Given the situation he had been in, Sharon wouldn't have liked knowing he was going to a strip bar, but may have been more tolerant if he had been up front about it. Sharon said to him:

> "Howie, to me a married man has no place in such a filthy, sleazy situation, and no real good can come of it. You knew how I felt about those kind of places before you went in with your buddies It's not as if I wish you would have called for permission since I'm not your mother. But the way you handled it left me questioning your integrity and how honest you are at other times. That undermines our connection and scares me."

Howie was definitely wrong to lie to Sharon. Whether he should have gone in or not may be debatable. If he promised he wouldn't, and did anyway, then he was out of integrity twice. It would be easy to waste a lot of time and energy looking at the situation as a lawyer might, trying to prove who was right and if there was adequate justification. By doing so, it's easy to overlook what results the couple really wanted to achieve and the process it would take to get there.

Sharon now felt insecure about her ability to know when her partner isn't telling the truth. She thought. "When else has he lied and I didn't know it?" Sharon wanted to feel more loved by Howie, and wanted to have trust in him. Instead she felt disrespected and insulted.

When Sharon became clear about what she was feeling, she was more able to articulate this to her husband. She expressed herself in a manner that had Howie understand her and also feel like making the effort to make the changes. This dramatically improved her chances of getting the desired results. In order to "travel more lightly," Sharon realized it would do neither of them any good if she was to hold this situation over his head indefinitely and try to squeeze mileage out of it. Getting back on track was more important to her.

They could easily have become distracted by arguing about whether it was really right or wrong for Howie to go into the bar. A lot of time could have been wasted trying to prove their points. The bottom line was Howie needed to show her he was genuinely sorry and that he really did care. He needed to convey that he respects her and he was truly sorry that he hurt her feelings, and he would try to not do so again.

Since Sharon sensed the authenticity of his comments and felt his words weren't empty promises, she began to forgive him. Without this it would've been much harder for her to let go of the anger, and her natural instinct may have been the use of punishment or the "doghouse."

Both partners play a significant role in abandoning the doghouse. It's much easier to forgive and move on with a sincere and heartfelt apology and the corresponding follow-through on actions promised.

While the story and the characters may be different, the concept of being in the doghouse happens in our neighborhoods everyday. The doghouse approach does not address the true problem, and instead creates a different set of problems of its own. When one partner becomes angry with the other, the ultimate goal is to achieve a correction of the problem and move back towards a connection with each other, not to get even with or to punish the one we love.

Some will still rely on the doghouse approach, which drags out the misery and feels like a ball and chain for both partners. If one person must be irritable, mean, distant and cold, and they stay that way for quite a while just so they can punish their partner, they aren't enjoying life during this time either. Besides, their partner may simply tune out the unpleasantness until it goes away. Chances are their partner might even rationalize their own behavior, and then *nothing* will really change. Put anyone in the doghouse too often, and they'll start looking for a warm home where someone will let them in.

Remember, we're not talking about who's right or wrong. That is almost always debatable. It's about how a couple handles problems when they occur. Dealing with problems as two rational adults who have matured beyond the punishment system is the key. The doghouse is a primitive tool that may keep your partner "under control" if that is what you want. Wouldn't you rather be a couple that played within a *mutually agreed upon* set of boundaries? Instead of fearing that you must play by the rules or you'd get punished, you both did so because you wanted to? This is an entirely different kind of relationship.

Chances are your partner will feel more respected if you stand firm in your convictions and talk about what happened, yet avoid resorting to "punishment." They'll usually love you more for being forgiving, and will be more motivated to not create that hurt again. If you desire to keep life together on the lighter side, let go of mistakes. Forgiving will serve you more than committing your partner to the infamous doghouse.

Waiting For Something To Happen

Pat and Crystal had their first child six months ago. Elisa, the new addition to the family, is the typical baby in that she requires a lot of time, care, and attention. Prior to her birth, Pat and Crystal's marriage was quite strong and showed no signs of weakness. However, lately Pat has been feeling abandoned and frustrated. He used to have a lot of time to spend with his wife. Now with Elisa on board, Crystal's attention and energy has shifted away from Pat and towards the new baby. Logically this makes sense to Pat, yet emotionally he feels left out.

As his insecurities became stronger, he began wondering if Crystal was bored and losing interest in him. Instead of bringing this problem up with her, Pat remained silent. During the weeks that passed, Pat felt increasingly ignored as Crystal appeared to be totally consumed by her new role as a mother.

Pat's resentment and fears continued to build, all the while he said nothing. Instead of talking about his feelings and his perception, Pat adopted the role of a private detective, and began to look for proof of the injustice being done to him. Every time Crystal did anything that could be interpreted by Pat as a gesture that further confirmed his fears, he said to himself, "Aha! I knew it. I knew she doesn't care about me anymore. What she just said or did proves it."

Many times people are *looking for proof* that their fears are accurate instead of communicating about their feelings. This sets the stage for their partner to fail as many comments and gestures will be mis-interpreted. We can become overly sensitive, awaiting any possible sign or gesture that suggests we are being wronged. In a sense we set a trap, waiting for our partner to fail so we can pounce and then prove our point.

> Pat asks Crystal what she wants to do for dinner. She doesn't hear him as she is focused on rocking the baby. "Aha! There's more proof," he thinks. After a few moments he gets her attention, and this time he asks her in a more irritable tone. Sensing his impatience, she responds "What is your problem? Can't you see I'm busy? *What do you want?*"

> Making dinner together used to be one of their most enjoyable activities, but not any more, at least since Elisa came along. Pat was growing more and more frustrated, and Crystal had no idea why. Little did she know that little incidents over the past few weeks have been convincing her husband that she doesn't love him very much any more, even though she loved him as much as ever.

Pat has been secretly watching "for something to happen" to confirm his feelings, fears, and beliefs. Instead of talking about it, he's been collecting proof, which means he's probably been mis-interpreting a wide variety of situations in order to find it. Pat's getting increasingly more upset over nothing. If he would share his thoughts and feelings with her, she could make some adjustments and be more aware of making sure he continues to feel her love and interest in him.

Often an emotional upheaval occurs because the one that was waiting for something negative to happen finally gets frustrated enough to go over the edge. This leaves the other thinking their partner is either losing their sanity or seriously blowing an incident out of proportion.

A healthier and more simple way to deal with our concerns is to just bring them up before we can find (or invent) proof.

If you don't know for sure but suspect or believe that your partner doesn't love you, respect you, or whatever the situation may be, and you don't confront it head on, you carry around a burden which is like a heavy weight on your shoulders. It helps to mention, when there is no conflict, that you're concerned about something. For example, you might mention to your partner that you're afraid they are taking you for granted, that you don't feel as loved and valued recently. Maybe you're just going through a period of insecurity or you're misinterpreting some comments or actions, but lately you've been worried a little about it.

Instead of saying to your partner, "You *are* more committed to your work or to our child than you are to me," why not say, "Lately I've been feeling that the child is taking most of your energy, and I want our relationship to always remain a priority. Sometimes I feel a little left out or ignored. I would love it if we could find more time together, just the two of us." Don't sit back and wait to build a case. Instead bring up your concerns when the feelings begin.

Bring up your concerns when you are noticing yourself looking for proof; don't wait until you find it.

Besides carrying an emotional burden, the danger in "waiting for it to happen" is that we regularly mis-interpreting things in order to be right and get our proof. The fact that Crystal got up early to take care of Elisa on Saturday morning instead of laying in bed with her husband doesn't mean that Elisa *is* more important than he is to her. But if he's looking for proof, waiting for it to happen, it becomes true. She may not even have known he wanted her to stay in bed, or how important it was to him that day.

You may not be totally wrong. Yet, why wait until there is in fact a problem, or until your partner has failed, or you've mis-interpreted a situation and gotten into a needless fight? Sometimes your gut feeling may be right, so bring it up then. Don't carry around your worries or start building up resentment. If you approach it like a lawyer and build a solid case, then your partner simply looks bad and you have a harder time keeping your relationship the source of love and renewal it can be.

Regaining The Spontaneity

Once a couple starts fighting and having problems on a consistent basis, one of the most difficult challenges they will face will be their ability to be spontaneous and have fun together. Often couples find it difficult to talk about anything other than their problems and frustration. To some it may seem silly to try having fun together because they need to "fix" their relationship first. They spend an enormous amount of time discussing or arguing about what is going wrong, and the pleasure and enjoyment they once derived from being together seems to evaporate.

When you came together at the beginning,
it wasn't so you could struggle with your partner.
You came together because of the positive
energy between the two of you.

At first you each saw the other as attractive and interesting and enjoyed each other's company. That needs to remain true in order for the relationship to last. When the fun and pleasure part disappears, the incentives or "benefits" are eliminated, and the relationship is stripped of its positive contribution to each of the partners. What is left is just a lot of work, frustration, and a skeleton of what once was, with only memories of good times.

Couples who find themselves in this endless loop of trying to "fix" their relationship need to find a way to break away from this task occasionally. They must set aside their problems and get back to having fun together. They must make time to be spontaneous and to enjoy each other's company again, which will give them more energy, help them become more interested in working a little harder, and encourage both to compromise.

By restoring positive energy they will renew their vision of why they wanted to work it out in the first place; because they have something worth saving. I'm not saying this is easy, or that you should totally abandon all constructive dialogue. Simply keep in mind that the better couples are at achieving balance, the stronger they become.

When I was a little boy, my mother would notice me becoming frustrated trying to build something or fix a toy. Being a determined kid who didn't like to give up or quit, I would stick with the project relentlessly, yet grow increasingly more agitated and ineffective. Mom would intervene and "strongly suggest" that I take a break and calm down. She'd say, "Come back to it later." I hated the advice then, but can see the timeless wisdom in it now. In a calmer state of mind I could return to the project with more clarity and resolve my problem much more quickly.

Communication is essential, but balance is important as well. If you can break out of the endless loop of needing to fix your problems together and instill some of the fun and enjoyment, it will make solving your issues much easier when you come back to them. Your spirit and energy will have changed and both of you will be more open and willing to listen and compromise.

If you can not attempt to have fun without bickering, arguing, or fighting, you need some counseling.

Chances are that whatever challenges you and your partner may be experiencing can be set aside momentarily. With the emotional support of a little fun and pleasure as a couple, you can regain your composure, put things into perspective more easily, and come back to talk about whatever is not working for you in your relationship a little easier.

One suggestion is to try making a list of fun activities that you both enjoy. You may want to include things that you've always wanted to do or have never done together. Also add to your list inexpensive activities that you can do on a daily basis as well as others that may need to be on the weekend or planned in advance. Make a conscious effort to incorporate these ideas into your life to put a little more pleasure and enjoyment back into being together.

Let's assume for a moment that you determined that you both could use a little break from your efforts to fix everything. It seems all you do is talk about "the two of you" when you are together. So you decide to go camping or on a short vacation. During your trip you continue the same conversations and fight over the same kinds of things. You would need to establish a truce for a while and change the subject.

When a group of people who work together go out with each other after work, naturally they usually slip into the rut of talking about work. It takes a concerted effort to keep the topic of conversation about things other than work, especially since that is often the most common denominator that they all share. When the conversation moves into something about work, someone needs to speak up and say, "Hey - let's not talk about work!" Everyone agrees and they can move onto talking about something else. You may need to do that among yourselves when you are together.

For couples who are entrenched in trying to solve their problems, give up the need to have everything fixed and resolved *now*. Otherwise you will no longer look forward to being together. Soon you will avoid each other, and begin living separate lives. All you will have left is "a lot of hard work."

Get a commitment from each other that the dialogue will continue, and set aside some future time to talk about your issues again. By simply lightening up and not always taking life and your relationship so seriously, you can resume being the interesting and fun person you once were and still can be.

~

Chapter 11

Hidden Treasures
Discovering the value of what's underneath conflict

~

What's Respect Got To Do With It?

Conflict is one of those aspects of life that most people want to avoid because frankly, it's not pleasant nor is being upset or angry much fun. Yet conflict has a hidden gift within it. When you understand what's at the bottom of what disturbed you or your partner, you find a shortcut to getting through the situation.

What pushes your buttons? What is it that really gets under your skin? If you are like most people, certain words, phrases, tones, expressions or looks can ignite a fire within you. A past partner of mine used to become infuriated when, during a tense conversation, I would unconsciously raise one eyebrow. Of course this was usually during a conflict. She interpreted this gesture to be a sign of smugness, which became the equivalent of putting a match to the fuse of a stick of dynamite.

My past partner accused me of never listening and being someone who was always right. As most everyone, I liked to be right, and back then there was probably some truth to her comments. Yet I liked to believe that I was reasonably open-minded, and those accusations seemed to be too absolute and all-encompassing. If she would have said, "It doesn't seem like you are listening," I could have gone along with it more than, "You *never* listen!" Her assertion that I could *never* be told anything suggested that I wasn't *ever* open to learning from anyone.

What angered me about her statements was the accusation *(by a person who supposedly loved me)* that I was broken and needed fixing. I didn't feel respected or given much credit. Instead, it appeared I had anything but her respect. Looking at what that "raised eyebrow" did to her - it's easy to assume that my "smugness" was an interpretation on her part *that I didn't respect her.*

Over the years I have become a better listener and much more open to other's ideas and perspectives. I'm sure my friend has grown and learned to communicate more effectively as well. My wife and I express ourselves in such a manner that we very rarely push each others buttons. But a lot of lessons were learned along the way.

I am not discouraged,
because every wrong attempt
discarded is another step forward.
Thomas Edison

Take heart, communicating and resolving conflict skillfully is not necessarily instinctive behavior. One of the keys to getting a handle on resolving conflict in your relationships is to understand the basis for it. In understanding what the fuel is that conflict needs to burn, you can, with clarity and efficiency, pinpoint what you need and want to change.

At the bottom of almost every conflict someone
doesn't feel loved, appreciated, respected, listened to, or understood.

Why do you get angry when your child doesn't do what you asked? Because you don't feel listened to or respected. You feel you are purposely being ignored. When your boss demands you work harder, but doesn't seem to notice or acknowledge how hard you've been working, you can become angry or resentful because you don't feel appreciated.

Of course, there are times when personalities just irritate you, or a car rudely pulls in front of you at an intersection and you become angry. But in personal conflicts between your partner and yourself you will almost always find that one or both of you doesn't feel respected, listened to, understood, appreciated or loved enough. When you recognize this, you will begin to articulate what is *really* wrong and get past the less important details of the conflict.

It was a hot Saturday afternoon, and Tom had spent most of the day painting the house. As he was moving his ladder, Tom accidentally broke the stalk of one of Vivian's rose bushes. She was furious, and gave him a passionate scolding. Tom naturally became defensive. Vivian made it sound as if he was an absolute loser who couldn't do *anything* right, and if he would only be a little more careful, he wouldn't *always* ruin or break things.

Tom had spent all day working hard on their house. He was not only tired of painting, but now he was being castigated because of a small accident. From his perspective, Vivian simply didn't appreciate his efforts. "Well, the hell with her," Tom concluded as he tuned her out. He didn't feel respected or appreciated.

The following weekend Vivian and Tom were going to a art festival. She was driving, and parking was scarce. They saw a spot but Vivian drove past it, concluding that it was just a little too small. Tom reacted loudly, questioning what she was doing. "There was a spot right there!" he said. She kept going since there were cars behind her and she couldn't back up. At the corner, Tom was thinking they should go straight, but instead she took a right turn. *"Now where are you going?!"* he yelled.

Beginning to get tired of his backseat driving, Vivian shouted back at him, "It's stressful enough trying to drive with all of this chaos and traffic. Would you please shut up and let me drive?!" They found a space, got out, and both were angry and not very talkative the rest of the day.

The real issue wasn't Vivian's driving or Tom's breaking of a rose bush. They could argue all day about who did or said what. The real issue in both situations was that because of their partner's comments *each person didn't feel respected* as a capable adult who was simply doing their best under the circumstances.

When you notice that you're upset, look to see what the underlying feeling is, and express that to your partner. This doesn't have to sound like June and Ward in "Leave It To Beaver." If you're clear, direct, to the point, and communicate without hostility, you'll be amazed at the results.

Here is what Vivian could have said:

> "Tom, I'm sure there are many things you'd do differently if
> you were driving. But you are not. I need your help, not your
> yelling. When you scream at me for not doing it your way, not
> only does it irritate me, but it makes me feel like you don't
> respect me as a capable driver much less as a person. Please try
> to be more patient when I'm driving."

All of these examples are simplistic for ease of illustration. Yet
many of the daily conflicts couples have are over small things. Even
little conflicts leave us feeling unloved, unappreciated, and anything but
closer to our partner.

> *Being able to see past the circumstances as to what is
> underneath is extremely valuable. It helps you express
> yourself clearly about the heart of the issue.*

Tom bought Vivian a food processor for her birthday. Vivian
became angry because she felt Tom didn't take the time to think
about what she would have really wanted. He had put very little
energy into expressing how important she was to him. Instead,
Tom merely stopped on the way home from work, bought the
food processor, and didn't even wrap it. He set it in the bag on
the table, receipt and all.

> *Ask for what you need.*

Vivian said, "Tom, I know you meant well by getting me the
blender. It's just that I can see you didn't spend much time,
other than stopping on the way home from work. When you
don't even wrap my gift, or even give me a card, it feels like
you just did your *duty*. And that's all. Because you didn't make
much of an effort, it doesn't seem like I'm very important enough
to you. I know those little details aren't as important to you,
and I know you love me, but I do wish you'd express it to me
more, especially on my birthday and holidays."

By removing the suggestion of hostile intent, and then expressing
what was missing, you can be heard without making your partner look

and feel bad. Your partner doesn't need to defend, and can *hear* that you didn't feel loved enough, regardless of what was intended. This conveys that you are not angry but just asking for it to be different the next time. Don't be hypocritical when expressing what you want from your partner. If you say you aren't feeling respected, express this in such a manner that still shows respect for them in return. If you say you don't feel listened to, then you should be willing to listen to your partner's response. When your comments suggest your partner is broken, screwed up, uncaring, or insensitive, it will be hard for him or her to hear you through your verbal attack.

The little conflicts add up over time,
and create a momentum in a relationship.

Avoid the temptation to argue about what happened. If you find yourselves caught up in this game that no one really wins, pull back and ask, "What is it that we are *really* fighting about?" This skill is very helpful in keeping conflicts in perspective. It keeps you focused on what you need to accomplish, and helps you avoid arguing about the interpretation each of you have about what happened. This reduces the possibility that a conflict will leave you both angry and distant.

Within your conflicts are opportunities to grow. When a smoke alarm is set off, the noise may be disturbing and unpleasant. Yet the prupose in getting your attention is served as it is quite impossible to ignore loudness. Obviously its not smart to take the batteries out of your smoke detector because you don't like the noise. Don't avoid conflcit at all costs because it's not pleasant. Instead look for the inherent gift.

Remember, at the bottom of almost every conflict, if you look closely enough you'll find at least one of you doesn't feel respected, appreciated, listened to, understood, or loved enough. That will give you the shortcut to get right to the heart of the issue instead of arguing about specifics. This helps both of you heal the wounds that were inflicted, making your connection with your partner stronger on a daily and long-term basis.

"Good breeding consists of concealing
how much we think of ourselves and
how little we think of the other person.
Mark Twain

Strengthening Your Emotional Bank Account

Imagine the concept of an emotional bank account in your relationship. Of course it doesn't actually exist in any physical sense, but it helps to visualize why some "small" issues create big problems.

Brandon has $10 in his bank account, and writes a $15 check. Not only would his check bounce, but his bank would penalize him just short of asking for his first child. His little $15 check creates a penalty of approximately $20 simply because there were not enough deposits to cover it.

Negative comments, coming home late, or not asking for your partner's input regarding an important decision may seem like small things but can certainly disintegrate the peace and start a battle when the emotional bank account between a couple is low. Little mistakes and other relatively minor bumps in the road to harmony for couples can be overcome much more easily when the "account" is full. The account is full when both partners feel connected, supported, loved, and appreciated.

Deposits are made when sweet things are done for each other. When we forgive someone easily and quickly. When we compromised or gave up what we wanted so our partner could have something they wanted. Deposits are made when we share intimacy and sincere affection and appreciation.

When the account is low, chances are very few deposits have been made. There is a tension in the relationship, similar to when you're broke and not sure where any new money might come from. Little things become big things and our patience grows thin.

Criticism, blame, or displays of disrespect are common withdrawals. When we fail to show acceptance, or consideration, or when we disregard our partner's needs and interests, we make withdrawals. When he fails to call, when she points out his weaknesses, when he makes fun of her in public, withdrawals are made.

When couples fight often, their emotional accounts are typically low. Little things set them off. By putting effort into making more deposits and strengthening the account, couples have more patience, become more willing to compromise, and forgive each other more easily.

If as a couple you are experiencing conflict on a regular
basis and seemingly little problems are constantly becoming big
problems, it is time to look at the ratio of deposits to withdrawals.

This is not about keeping a ledger. The objective is not to destroy the spontaneity and "friendliness" of your actions. Don't try to keep a balance sheet. Just strive to make more and more daily deposits. Avoid making excuses or rationalizing inconsiderate or hostile actions by telling yourself you "can afford a few withdrawals." Acknowledge withdrawals as such when you make one, and genuinely apologize.

Remember, it is irrelevant if you think the account is strong
if your partner doesn't feel the same way.

There's no "master" account because each of us have our own perception. And there's no real way of reaching a safe balance. You don't become a "billionaire" to where your relationship can withstand any withdrawal. Things like adultery or abuse can wipe out years of "savings" and leave your emotional account bankrupt.

Have you been helpful lately? Patient? Understanding? Appreciative? If so, you're making deposits, and keep up the good work! Have you been lazy, short-tempered, sarcastic, or critical lately? If so, it's time to stop bleeding the account and begin making more deposits. Thank each other for the deposits. Acknowledge when you or your partner has made a withdrawal.

Keep no notes, hold no mental list. Just commit to making more and more deposits and creating a strong emotional connection between you. Share why you love each other and regularly acknowledge the contribution your partner is to your life. Make it fun if you can. Do it to be silly, to be a friend, or to be a caring partner.

Remember, underneath most conflict between couples there is someone who isn't feeling loved enough, respected, appreciated, understood, or listened to. You have the ability to avoid arguing about specifics and approach the "real" problem. The conflicts that arise from a low account have a gift within them. Remember that a "low bank account" usually means there are significant deficiencies in one or more of these areas, and by talking with your partner, you will know specifically where your efforts need to be directed.

~

"Don't lose time in conflict; time can never be recovered."
Unknown

~

CHAPTER 12

The Bridge Between Two Partners
Why communication is a couple's friend

~

The Importance Of Communication

When asked what the most challenging area of their relationship is, most couple's response is "communication." Why is this basic part of life so vital yet so challenging? Because it's the link between a couple in their day-to-day life together. Messages are constantly being sent back and forth while in each other's presence.

Our communication reveals our thoughts and feelings about our partner. The verbal and non-verbal communication between two people can have an incredibly powerful impact, leading to an emotional connection or distance, to laughter or tears.

Our words are especially potent as within them
lie the messages of how we either like or dislike,
respect or loathe, admire or despise our partner.

We typically don't realize that we are communicating such strong messages. Yet at every moment our words are interpreted and often carry much more significance than we think. What we say, accidentally or not, can and often does lead to hurt feelings and deep emotional wounds.

For example, imagine a man says to his wife, "Don't you understand how to set the timer? Do I need to show you *again*?!" His words, tone, and facial expression convey he believes his partner is ignorant and a slow learner, which obviously does not bring them closer as a couple.

Sometimes you may hurt your partner by off-hand, *seemingly* insignificant comments. You may anger the one you love by accusing them of being stupid or unattractive. You might indirectly say that you feel they aren't trying hard enough, they're irresponsible, or you think they need to change. Occasionally you may blame or accuse your partner, or you may not give them a break for their imperfections - all with your words, tone of voice, and facial expressions.

> *"A good marriage would be between*
> *a blind wife and a deaf husband."*
> Michel de Montaigne

Although you usually don't intend to hurt, wound, or show disrespect to your partner, sometimes you still may do so. Your words are like paintings, left to be interpreted, and too many times may result in misunderstandings.

What you think you are saying is often not what your partner thinks you are saying. Your tone of voice can distinctly change the message you intend to express. Sometimes your body language contradicts or further defines what you're trying to say, such as rolling your eyes, folding your arms, or clenching your jaw. Non-verbal communication sends important signals which your partner must also *interpret*, increasing the possibility of misunderstandings.

Your partner is hearing and looking at the entire communication package, and from that viewpoint they decide what all of your messages mean. Communication between your partner and yourself can just as easily create distance and separation as a spirit of understanding and togetherness.

Both partners need to acknowledge the essential role that communication plays in a relationship, and would each greatly benefit by striving to improve their skills in this area.

The Benefit Of Learning More About Communicating

Some people say, "Why do I *have* to learn how to communicate more effectively with my partner, my children, or my employees at work? I should just be able to say what I think or feel!" It is essential to understand that it's not that you *have* to learn how to communicate more effectively. Doing so simply improves the possibility that you will achieve the results you are striving for, regardless of whether you want to see your partner make some changes or you simply want to have rapport between you.

In the last few chapters on conflict, many potential issues which couples often fight about were mentioned. Partners who can't resolve their problems usually don't stay together very long. Strong communication skills help couples get through these situations together.

By being able to communicate intelligently, you have a gift and a tool that will serve you well in many circumstances. A little thoughtfulness, diplomacy, and tact does not make you manipulative, but rather better at expressing yourself so people can not only hear you, but actually listen to what you have to say without being offended or becoming defensive.

The idea is not to learn new "techniques," but rather to change your perspectives and approaches to create more receptivity to what you have to say to each other. It's not as important to know the "right" words or phrases to use as having a good underlying attitude which is expressed.

Your words are only a vehicle to convey how you feel.
The emotion that you feel shapes the words you choose and how you use them. When you approach your partner with genuine caring and love, your words and phrases take on less significance.

Your ability to communicate well improves the odds that you will be successful in your endeavor to have a satisfying, long-term relationship. You can improve the possibility that you will be listened to and understood. It's not just a matter of speaking your mind that makes you a good communicator. A little finesse can make all of the difference between just getting your point across and actually getting the results that you desire.

How You Communicate Does Make A Difference

I'll always remember a couple who said, "We have no problem communicating. We say exactly what's on our minds!" Unfortunately what they did say often did more damage than it did good, and they fought constantly. How a couple communicates has a lot to do with their effectiveness in dealing with the issues at hand, and shapes how they feel about each other in the process and afterwards.

Many people avoid taking responsibility for their attempts at communication, and disregard the role they play in the actions, attitudes, and behaviors of those around them. For example, some teachers might blame society, parents, and the students themselves for their lack of attentiveness and interest. While these explanations may hold true for some, a great teacher will be able to reach the majority of students by being captivating and entertaining. They relate the information in a concise way, and also make it meaningful and memorable through their proficiency in communication.

I've heard many people tell me their partners were not good at communicating, while being quite unaware of their own limitations and ineffective approaches. Instead of worrying about fixing their partner's supposed inability to communicate, these people were often better served by looking at their own strengths and weaknesses for ways to improve.

The Power Of Words

What makes the difference between one sports team's inspiring coach versus an opponent's apparent lack of leadership? What makes one teacher outstanding while the others simply go through the motions? What makes one lawyer so convincing in the courtroom compared to their counterpart? Why is one parent listened to and another ignored?

The major tool these people rely upon is their ability to communicate in a manner that impacts others. Their words resonate, create interest, captivate, and inspire. It's not the number of words a person knows, but how they use them that can separate one from the masses. Most believe they have little to learn about communication, yet distance themselves from their lovers, alienate employees, discourage their children, bore their students, or deflate the team they coach.

"The more we know, the more we want to know;
when we know enough,
we know how much we don't know."
Carol Orlock

The very nature of most human beings is linked to freedom. We are an animal that does not do well in solitude or captivity. Most resist and resent being ordered, forced, and coerced. If your communication implies that your partner is wrong, or has no choice but to follow your commands, the typical instinctive reaction from your partner will probably be a stubborn and defiant resistance.

Instead of trying to force your partner to change, to talk with you, to help more, or respond in any fashion that you desire, your words can instead motivate, inspire, or persuade. Very rarely can you *force* anyone to do anything. The only tool you really have is your ability to communicate in manner that encourages the listener to respond in the manner you desire.

Imagine that your neighbor has a teen-ager who they'd like to have cut the grass. After repeated requests, their son refuses to get off the couch to do the job. The parent could threaten to punish their child by taking away phone privileges, not allowing them to see their friends for a week, or withholding their allowance. Yet none of these approaches to discipline can provide a *guarantee* that the grass will get cut.

The better you are at relating to other people,
the better you get at not only seeing the results you desire,
but also establishing and maintaining solid relationships
that are based upon mutual respect and admiration.

The parent may eventually get their teen to do it by screaming and yelling, but they might find their rose bushes have been run over with the mower as a result. Yet if the parent is persuasive enough, the grass could get cut properly without using blackmail, punishment, or paying their son off. The idea is to communicate skillfully and effectively so the intended result is accomplished *without any anger or hostile feelings between them.*

The Importance Of What You Don't Actually Say

All of us send many messages through our expressions, tone of voice, or our posture. Instinctively and intuitively we are usually aware of the messages being sent to us from others. Even when we sense someone doesn't want to talk to us, we rarely think, "I can see they don't want to talk. They are leaning away from me, with their arms folded, and they have been getting restless in the last few minutes." Yet we still pick up the message.

We send an unbelievable amount of unintentional messages to those around us, yet very few of us are aware of the messages we are sending *as we are sending them.* When confronted with them, sometimes we may become defensive because we "never said that." Since these messages are usually being silently interpreted by another person, non-verbal communication stands the greatest chance of being misinterpreted.

If you are in a long-term relationship, however, give your partner credit for knowing you well enough to pick up on some of the non-verbal cues that you send. If they are wrong about them, simply clarify how you are feeling instead of criticizing them for misinterpreting your non-verbal cues.

Chances are good that your partner will pick up on that subtle rolling of the eyes. They will detect the clenched jaw. They may sense your impatience by your restlessness. They've seen you cross your arms before when you were being stubborn! And your partner will probably know that even though you said nothing, your silence may mean you're either angry or wounded.As the observer of your partner's non-verbal cues, be careful to not make all of your interpretations "true." For example, imagine that Dean was talking to his new wife, Marie.

As he looked at her posture, he noticed she was leaning away from him, with her arms folded and legs crossed. She was getting restless and was looking around the room. Would it be *true* that she was irritated with Dean? While those non-verbal signs could suggest that she was, this interpretation could be completely inaccurate since she may actually just have to go to the restroom! When you don't talk about what you perceive, you may decide that your interpretation of their actions is true.

If your partner was hurt or upset by what you said, yet you thought your words should not have created this reaction, you may want to ask yourself, "Am I doing something that may be causing this reaction? Is it what I said, how I said it, or my body language?" Arguing about what you said will get you nowhere.

Remember, you send countless non-verbal messages without trying to. When someone gets to know you well enough, he/she will eventually start becoming aware of what the non-verbal messages mean that you send regularly. If you and your partner seem to have many misunderstandings, you may need to look beyond just the words that you use to all of the messages you are sending to each other.

Clarity Makes Finding Your Way Possible

Try to find your way around Chicago with a map of New York. Obviously the experience would be frustrating and impossible. Similar to a road map, clear and direct communication can truly help a couple navigate through the peaks and valleys of their relationship more easily.

Communication can be your best friend since it connects you and your partner, and can help you to continually strengthen your relationship. It provides you each with information on how you can both become better partners for each other. Your ability to communicate helps you both be aware of where you are heading and how you can stay on track as a couple.

When you avoid talking about problems, hoping they'll go away or your partner will forget about them, you not only fail to set a clear direction for the future, but you also usually end up on the same dead end streets over and over later on. If you are driving and notice you're lost, it's smart to pull over and get directions. The longer you wait, the more possibility that you will go much further out of your way.

Many couples will procrastinate and wait to discuss an issue until the problem can not be discussed without anger or hostility. When they finally get around to talking, they are sometimes afraid to be direct, honest, and to the point. They may drop hints, make sarcastic comments, or express their frustration or concerns in a manner that discourages a productive and positive conversation. Clear, direct, and friendly communication is the road map which can help them get back on track.

Sometimes couples avoid talking about important issues or problems in their relationships because of their past experiences trying to do so. Their memories of misunderstandings, conflicts, and hurt feelings may stand in their way as they are reluctant to go through all of that again. They don't trust the fact that they could do it without getting the same old results. By using a new approach with a more positive attitude couples *can* talk about challenging topics in a more mature and open-minded manner.

Being able to clearly express your thoughts, feelings,
and needs, without putting your partner on the defensive,
can help any couple get back and stay on track.

Clear and direct communication does not have to be blunt and abrasive. It's important to keep your partner's spirit open to hearing you without becoming angered or wounded. Instead of your comments being perceived as attacks, what you have to say can be interpreted as being motivated by your love for your partner and your desire for your relationship to be what you both want and need for it to be.

Throughout their marriage, Dean and Marie have had their share of challenges. They have come a long way in their ability to communicate effectively. When they first started out, Dean was often direct but abrasive. Marie would often get her feelings hurt by the way Dean said things. Not wanting to be hurtful in return, Marie was non-confrontational but very indirect in her approach to communication. Both have learned how they could use the best aspect of each other's approaches.

Dean worked sixty hours a week, while Marie's schedule was from nine to five. He used to always find a way to spend time with her, but now he was always working. When they first were married, Marie was very indirect. When she was feeling taken for granted, Marie would say, "You sure are working a lot lately. Don't you get tired of being away from the house so much?" Dean would reply, "Not at all. I like what I'm doing." She would hint further, "I was thinking you might like to take a class or join a co-ed team with me in the evenings." "I'm just too busy to take something like that on right now." he'd say.

The conversation would be over and Dean would have no idea that his wife was lonely and missed him, and she was afraid that this trend would only get worse in the future. Today the way they express themselves is much different. Marie would instead say:

"You really have been working a lot lately, and you seem to really enjoy it. I miss you, but I also know your work is very important to you, and you're great at what you do. Because I don't make a big deal about you being gone so much, you don't seem to think twice about it.

Sometimes I'm afraid that your work is more important to you than I am. I don't want that to come between us, and I don't imagine you want that either. All I really need is to know that I can count on having at least three or four nights a week with you, where you come home around dinner time and we can spend the evening together."

Being clear is simply stating your feelings, thoughts, and what you want. There's no need to make this complicated by listing "ten steps" to follow. Avoid "testing" your partner by hinting around. If you've got something to say, say it directly, yet with respect and caring. By not making your partner defensive and by simply stating what the "real issue" is at hand, you can clearly and precisely express yourself to your partner.

With some clarity about where you both need to head, it is easier for a couple to respond accordingly. If you both make a regular habit of being clear and direct, you can continually tune your relationship and make minor adjustments as you go, helping you stay on track.

Communication is the most important bridge for couples to use in getting past the challenges and issues in their relationship. Your honesty and openness is your road map to where you both really want to go together, and by doing this throughout your years together you will find your relationship becoming even stronger than when you first fell in love.

In the next chapter we'll look more closely at how you can immediately begin to improve your chances of getting through to each other.

~

"Things do not change; we change"
Henry David Thoreau

~

Chapter 13

Easy Listening
Making it easier for your partner to hear you

~

Improving Your Chances Of Being Understood

Although below the surface, within some of our communications are unintentional messages such as, "you're an idiot and I know everything." A skillful communicator is careful to not pass these undesirable messages to his or her partner, knowing it is in their mutual best interest to be listened and understood. To illustrate how you can express yourself without hints of negativity, consider this example from Tim & Erin:

"Tim, I know you've been working hard lately and have helped around the house by doing some of the big projects like cutting the grass and painting the fence. It's just that today I'm feeling exhausted, and it seems like there's still so much to do around here. Even though you already help a lot, I really could use a little more help. I have to run the kids downtown this afternoon and was hoping you'd help me with the dishes and by throwing a load of laundry in for me."

Erin acknowledged Tim for his efforts. He wasn't being told he's been lazy, and can be the hero for helping out instead of just doing his "fair share." Instead of an indirect statement that is vague about needing more help, Erin made it clear how he could help, and *she kept her request friendly and reasonable.* She attained what she wanted without a fight. Tim helped willingly, and afterwards, when Erin thanked him for helping, he quietly decided he needed to help her more and now does so regularly.

You can be listened to, understood, and get the results you desire without complaining, blaming, or using obligation, duty, or guilt.

Tim and Erin never got into a battle over whether he did or did not help out enough. Since there was no implied negativity, Tim never became defensive. Instead, Erin simply expressed her message that she needed help, and because of her approach, without a struggle, he felt inclined to do so. By using a more diplomatic approach in the first place, she stood a greater chance of getting the intended results without ruffling his feathers. Chances are Tim never even thought about her approach. He simply responded to a non-threatening, non-accusational request from someone he cares about and wants to help.

Learn a little finesse and elegance, and everyone wins.

Because of the lack of any negative messages hidden within her words, Tim willingly helped out. If Erin would have used the guilt approach, it would have been very hard for him to feel empathy because he would have been busy defending himself. He would probably have become more focused on being right than on understanding how she felt and what she wanted.

Anytime you catch yourself blaming your partner, accusing them, or applying a guilt or obligation routine, remember that it makes it harder for your partner to remain emotionally neutral and open to your comments or requests. We'll cover the topic of making requests in more detail in chapter 16. A little thought, consideration, & a shift in attitude can help you communicate in a more supportive, loving manner.

The key to this negative-free approach is a positive shift in attitude in regards to who your partner is to you. Keep in mind how important and valuable this person is to you while you are expressing yourself and you will *begin* communicating differently. Remembering how much you love and appreciate your partner can shape the way you approach him/her about sensitive issues.

Intentionality

Almost every time you become frustrated, angry, or hurt by what your partner says, you can move through and past it faster by recognizing that chances are he/she had no intention of upsetting you. Your partner probably didn't sit down and plot ways to attack you while eating breakfast that morning.

Tim and Erin initially experienced some problems after their first child. Erin had become frustrated with Tim's apparent inability to learn what she had shown him regarding caring for their baby. For example, once Tim had been trying to feed the baby for fifteen minutes and was making very little progress when Erin said impatiently, "Tim, don't you know how to feed a baby *yet*?!" Her tone and selection of words suggested that Tim was an incompetent father. Although Erin did not *intend* to offend him, she did.

Tim took a deep breath and remembered that her selection of words and tone of voice was not deliberate or thought out well in advance. Of course, no one would like to be talked to that way. Yet Erin had no conscious intention of striking out at him. Tim kept this in mind as he responded to her without hostility.

"Erin, I know you didn't mean to insult me. But the way you just said that to me left me feeling like a little boy being scolded by his mother. I know you meant well, and you probably get frustrated with teaching me all of these things. But I do want to learn, and I need you to try to be patient and helpful instead of criticizing." Erin thought for a moment about what Tim said and responded by saying, "I am sorry Tim. I didn't intend to bark at you. I'll try to be more patient."

Since words are typically a reflection or expression of what's going on inside our minds, when the wrong selection of words is used, it can really hit a nerve. In the example with Tim and Erin, if he hadn't been thoughtful in his response, he could have easily escalated the situation by becoming angry with her.

Tim blundered one day by saying to Erin, "Honey, that outfit makes you look old." He wasn't trying to hurt her feelings. Yet she was feeling a little sensitive about getting older. Even though Tim should know better than to make such a remark, the real lesson is that Tim was speaking his truth and meant no harm.

Erin remembered the principle of "intentionality," and responded by saying, "Tim, I'm sure you didn't mean to say *I look old*, but that's how I heard it and it hurt my feelings. Do you really think I look old?" Even though Erin let her partner know she was wounded, this kind of response was possible because she remembered intentionality. If she hadn't, Erin may have become upset and responded with a much less loving comment such as, "Well, your beer belly isn't exactly turning me on!" and then a fight may have ensued.

Being 100% honest and open (or blunt and tactless) with each other isn't always possible, desirable, or even in our mutual best interest. Men are typically very literal and often quite direct, and sometimes fail to consider the many interpretations and consequences possible before speaking.

If your partner makes the mistake of upsetting you, before you respond consider whether or not they intended to do so. You don't need to just turn the other cheek, but you may be able to not become as angered or hurt as you may otherwise be.

The key to remember is that the majority of what comes out of your partner's mouth is not *meant* to hurt or anger. There is no doubt times when our messages can be better stated with a little finesse so as to not inflict wounds or "push another's buttons." But we don't live in a perfect world, and our partner may occasionally use a choice of words that accidentally leaves us wounded. It is in these moments that we need all the strength we can muster to find the ability to keep in mind the principle of intentionality.

The fact that our partner's words were never intended to hurt us doesn't make what was said O.K., but it does increase the possibility we will be able to keep things somewhat in perspective.

Accepting Your Partner's Reality

As discussed in the above section, occasionally errors are made in your communications with your partner. Tim accidentally offended his wife Erin by telling her she looked old in the outfit she was wearing. In situations such as this, both would be better off if she expressed her feelings and also forgave Tim without making an enormous issue out of his blunder. Yet it may not always be so easy to do so. Sometimes one partner becomes upset and the other doesn't share their anger, hurt, or frustration. If Erin hadn't been as understanding and instead became resentful towards Tim, chances are he would have become defensive rather than apologetic. Since Tim knew he hadn't intended to hurt her feelings, he would have then believed she had misinterpreted his comment and was over-reacting.

Instead of invalidating Erin's feelings, Tim said to her "I'm sorry I upset you with that last comment. I didn't mean to. I think we're both a little sensitive about getting older, I know I am. I still find you to be beautiful, and you don't look old to me at all." Just by acknowledging her feelings and apologizing, Tim healed the small wound before it became any worse.

If you were to say to your partner, "When you don't pick up after yourself around the house I feel taken for granted" you would be expressing what that gesture means to you, regardless of whether it was intended or not. Another example is, "When you told me that you're afraid I will forget to pick up the kids after school I felt like you were saying I can't be depended on." How a situation is experienced by *your partner is what needs to be acknowledged and dealt with.*
An obviously ineffective approach would be, "You're all wrong. You misinterpreted what I said. It's your fault, not mine. I never said that and never intended that." Here you invalidate your partner's feelings. You basically tell them you played no part in their interpretation. This is not a very diplomatic and congenial way to get to where you want to go. Accept some responsibility, apologize for sending a message that resulted in your partner's feelings being hurt, and heal the wound.

The bottom line is what your *partner is feeling is what they're feeling.* It isn't right or wrong. Their reactions, feelings, or actions may seem unreasonable, unnecessary, or inappropriate. It may not have been the way you would have reacted, or the way you would have *liked them to.* Yet that's irrelevant. *How they feel is how they feel.*

> *"Every issue, belief, attitude, or assumption*
> *is precisely the issue that stands between you*
> *and your relationship to another human being."*
> Gita Bellin

Never tell your partner, "You shouldn't be angry. You need to get over it," or, "You're over-reacting." The odds are good that he/she will take offense to your presumption that you know what and how they should be feeling.

Too many times we get so hurt or angry by our partner's selection of words that the conversation takes an unfortunate turn. The couple finds themselves becoming increasingly upset when the conflict could have been diffused at the very beginning. You can reduce the possibility of "escalation" by remembering intentionality, and then by not invalidating your partner's feelings with comments such as "You're making a big deal out of nothing."

> *It's valuable to learn how to express yourself,*
> *but it's just as important to change the way you look*
> *at the comments, actions, and feelings of your partner.*
>
> *Your new attitude will be reflected in your words,*
> *tone of voice, and body language.*

There are no "right" words or phrases to memorize. Instead what is essential is the shift in attitude which is reflected by your words. If you are sincere, your partner will get the message that you are indeed sorry and you do care. This helps make it much easier to let go of hurt or frustration and move on. When your words feel "empty" to your partner, as if they are being read out of a book, he/she will easily detect the lack of sincerity.

Recently Kris asked me if I would clean up the kitchen after she left for a meeting. I agreed, and then proceeded to get involved in other projects and forgot all about it. I didn't intentionally disregard her request. It was an honest oversight. However, when she came home, nothing had been done. She felt that I had ignored her request and felt taken for granted because recently I had not been showing much initiative in doing the household tasks.

Thankfully, Kris was able to bring this up in a manner that didn't leave me feeling defensive. There was no need to go to great lengths to explain my forgetfulness. She wanted a little help, I said I would do so, and then didn't.

Kris said, "I was disappointed when I came home tonight and saw the kitchen was a mess. I don't ask for your help cleaning up the kitchen very often, and you didn't follow through. I'm sure you didn't plan on not doing it, but either way, it still didn't get done." I heard her loud and clear. She didn't get upset, but was firm and didn't ignore the situation. I didn't waste time acknowledging that not only had I let her down, and hadn't been helping very often, but I was genuinely sorry as well.

The next day, while she was out doing errands, I did the dishes, vacuumed, swept the floors, cleaned the countertops, did laundry, took out the garbage, and dusted. All as a gesture to express my genuine apology. She was impressed, and I was proud of myself. A weak apology is one that is just words but never results in any change of behavior or action taken.

My lack of original follow through wasn't a big problem from my perspective. Yet even though Kris didn't get upset, it was much more significant to her. Because of that, I acknowledged her feelings and took measures to show her I understood. I'm certainly not the perfect partner at all times, but in this one example, you can see how I take my relationship seriously enough to listen to my partner's concerns, and do what it takes to show I love her and I care.

You can do the same by acknowledging your partner's "reality" as being just as valid and important as your own. Pay attention to how your actions, words, and non-verbal communication effect your partner. Respond accordingly when a misunderstanding occurs.

Keeping Your Perspective

Some of the most common misunderstandings are simply poorly worded communications between a couple. It really doesn't matter all that much what was actually said or done. If you want to waste a lot of time and energy, argue all day about what *really* happened and what was really said. Instead, try to keep the situation in perspective by not allowing a minor problem to escalate.

Ron and Jill have been living together for 5 years. One day Ron came home later than planned for dinner. He hadn't called, and Jill grew increasingly upset as her carefully prepared dinner became overcooked. She felt he was becoming incredibly inconsiderate and much too involved in his work. Jill wondered if Ron was losing interest in her.

Ron had been anxious about being late, and tried getting out of the office early. But his boss cornered him for 45 minutes when he had been preparing to leave. When Ron tried to call home, the phone was busy, so he just left the office. Along the way home he'd thought about finding a pay phone and calling Jill, but then decided against it since the line may still have been busy, and stopping would set him back another 10 minutes. This is how they handled the situation after he had returned home:

Jill: "Where the hell have you been? Why were you late again? Why didn't you have the common decency to at least call?"
Ron: "I've been at work, making money to pay for things around here. What are you so upset about?"
Jill: "Dinner is ruined because you were late again. I'm sick of it. Is your job all that matters to you anymore?"
Ron: "Give me a break would you!? I work hard all day and I walk in the door and you start nagging me! What's the big deal?"
Jill: "You were an hour late, and you didn't even call! You think I like spending all this time cooking so I can just throw it out?"
Ron: "I wasn't an hour late! I was 45 minutes late. I *did* call you, but the phone was busy. I wanted to hurry and get home so you wouldn't be mad again. If I would've sat around waiting..."

Jill: "What do you mean, so I wouldn't get mad again? You make it sound like it's all my fault, that I just get mad over nothing!"

Ron: "That's not what I said!"

Jill: "That's what you meant."

Ron: "Well, you have to admit, you do get upset a lot."

Jill: "Well, that's because you're a jerk a lot!"

There is obviously a better way. Chances are there was originally no hostility or viciousness intended by each partner. They only wanted their partner to understand and acknowledge that their perspective was valid. If they didn't blow the situation out of proportion, they could have addressed the heart of the matter and proceeded through it more quickly and easily. Consider the following "alternate" approach:

Jill: "Hi, Ron, I'm glad you're home."

Ron: "Hi ,Jill. Sorry I'm late."

Jill: "Thanks. You know Ron, I'm sure you didn't try to be late, or try to aggravate me, but I hate to tell you that dinner is quite ruined. I wish you would have called me. What happened?"

Ron: "The boss cornered me as I was leaving and talked for 45 minutes. Then when I called, the phone was busy."

Jill: "You know, lately I've worried that you're losing interest in spending time with me, and that work is becoming more important to you. Tonight I was getting kind of angry when I hadn't heard from you. The salad was getting soggy and the roast dried out, and you still weren't home."

Ron: "I'm sorry, Jill. I wanted to be home on time. I didn't know you've been feeling that way lately. Maybe I am working a little too much. I'll make more of an effort to be home earlier, and to let you know when I think I'm going to be late. Thanks for not jumping on me when I got in the door."

Instead of arguing about the facts or expanding the issue into other subjects, Ron heard her concerns, and she could see that in his response. She made it easier for him to not get defensive by not accusing him of any hostile intent. But she also didn't shy away from telling him what was on her mind.

Your point does not have to be proven to be understood.

In the second approach Jill's odds were much better of getting what she really wanted, which wasn't to have Ron feel like a failure, but to simply be more considerate in the future. What made this more possible was her ability to keep things in perspective from the beginning. Jill was able to express with clarity what the bottom line was regarding why she was actually upset and what she wanted to be different next time.

You can and will improve your chances of being listened to and understood if you remove any messages of negativity. Conflicts can be avoided by keeping things in perspective, remembering the concept of intentionality, and showing a respect and appreciation for your partner's reality. In the next chapter you will discover how the way you communicate can create a positive shift in your attitudes and feelings about your partner.

~

Chapter 14

Trading Places

A change in perspective can lead to a change of heart

~

Creating Understanding Instead Of Agreement

While I may see a particular celebrity as a confident leader, you might see the same person as arrogant and pretentious. I may think Rome is an interesting place, you might think it is too crowded, expensive, and unfriendly. You may enjoy eating raw octopus, while I find it to be rubbery and unappealing. We could talk all day, but I may never come to agree with you or you with me.

Throughout our lives we all look at some of the same things very differently. In our own minds, we truly believe that *we are right.* Having differences of opinion or perspectives is natural and healthy for couples. However, problems usually arise when one partner needs to change the other's perception. The purpose of communication is not to achieve agreement. Rather it is about sharing who you are; what you feel, think, and believe. You can express yourselves in order to simply establish a greater mutual understanding of each other.

With this notion that we must convince our partners that our perspective is more accurate, we often set ourselves up for failure and frustration. My experience with couples has shown me that this is one of the most common daily struggles. Yet, so many people don't recognize their own tendency to argue about who's right, and instead believe it's their partner who always thinks and acts as if *they're* right.

Communication may help you persuade another to take action or change in some way. It can help you get close to people and develop long-term friendships. It can help you solve problems. It can entertain you. But the purpose of communication, especially when it comes to couples, is not to get the other to see that you're right and they aren't. Couples who give up always trying to be "right" and willingly agree to disagree argue much less.

When we first start dating it often is an admirable trait that this new person in our life has a different outlook. But as the years pass many people expect their partner to shadow their beliefs, feelings, and perceptions, and can become quite upset when they don't. The subjects that begin the arguments could be anything from politics to parenting. Regardless, it's hard for most couples to just calmly agree to disagree.

Some partners can honestly look at the other and say, "I didn't know you felt that way. I personally don't feel that way." Period. Two partners can understand each other without agreeing. They can experience no negative feelings about their differences in belief, attitude, or perception, and aren't concerned if they don't agree at all times. This allows the two people to walk away from disagreements without any anger or hostile feelings towards each other.

While this may be easy to do with some subjects, it's not always going to be enough to agree to disagree when some compromise or decisions need to be arrived at. When this is the case, couples will still benefit from avoiding the urge to "prove their point" and be right.

By trying to more amicably consider each other's perspective and form a consensus, the stance taken will have a lot to do with their partners' openness to their ideas and way of seeing the situation. Remember, you're on the same team, and a rigid "you have no idea what you're talking about" attitude only encourages resistance and rigidity in return.

The Reverse Play

Another typical response that frequently occurs in communication between couples is what I refer to as the "reverse play." Instead of hearing what one's partner has to say, a person avoids taking their partner's comments to heart by always turning the situation around, thus avoiding responsibility. The following is an example that will illustrate this further:

Adam is a master at reversing the focus and making a situation appear as if Beth's shortcomings are to blame whenever she is upset or frustrated with him. He gets off the hook by building a case that her perspective is flawed. He rarely can admit to being less than perfect. Even worse, she gets no actual results from her original requests for change.

Beths says, "Adam, you don't help out enough around the house. It's not fair, I have to take care of the kids and do all of the cleaning, and I'm exhausted." Adam responds with, "That's not true, I do plenty. Just yesterday I washed the cars. Don't blame me because you're tired. If you didn't let the kids make such big messes and allow everything get so chaotic you wouldn't be so tired of cleaning up."

Adam shifts Beth into believing she is looking at the situation incorrectly. Subconsciously, Adam assumes Beth will see that he has great wisdom and she's in fact responsible and the one that should change. If he can shift his partner's thinking to agree with his perspective, he doesn't have to change or do anything differently. Since Adam, like most of us, usually believes that he is right, this allows him to not feel manipulative.

While this may work in getting Beth to back off of her request for more help, it doesn't do much to strengthen their partnership and sense of being a team, much less support feelings of intimacy and closeness between them.

Agreeing to disagree helps you avoid wasting a lot of energy arguing about differences in taste, perception, and beliefs. Yet when there is an obstacle in your relationship that must be dealt with, such as Beth's concern about having more help around the house, in order to move in a positive direction, it helps to have a spirit of flexibility and openness to your partner's concerns.

The reverse play keeps a couple stuck in the same situation with no real progress. You may not always agree, but as a loving partner you will still make the effort to make sure your partner feels listened to, respected, and loved. If Adam cared more about being that kind of partner for Beth, he would willingly choose to help her more even if he thought that he already helped enough.

Beth tells her husband, "You rarely initiate sex anymore. Are still attracted to me?" Since Adam never takes responsibility, he finds something or someone to blame. He redirects the focus to her by saying, "I got tired of initiating only to have you passively respond. Besides, you never initiate either!"

Many relationships exist in which one of the partners is very controlling. How is this "controlling" achieved? Through clever manipulation that results in one person believing the other must always be listened to, obeyed, or "respected." This controlling person is often unfair, selfish, and egotistical, which helps him/her be successful in assuming a leadership role within the relationship. This "controller" is also usually a master at the reverse play and convincing his/her partner most everything that is a problem is really the partner's fault.

Sure, most of us don't like to look bad and it is especially hard to take responsibility for our less-than-admirable behavior or action. We hate being blamed, and even when the accusations are true, we tend to look for ways to shift the blame or explain away our responsibility. However, couples who strive to give up use of the "reverse play" will begin listening to one another and acknowledging each other's perspectives like never before.

As you begin to acknowledge your partner's perspective, your feelings towards them will in turn be more loving and accepting. This creates an opening for movement and growth, both of which are necessary for the long-term success of a relationship.

Your Own Reflection

People are like mirrors to us. They show us what they feel about what we have said or done by the faces they make, their body language, and the words they choose in response. Life isn't black or white. We're all interpreted in thousands of different ways by different people.

Imagine an American tourist who is impatient and demanding. They go to France and leave believing the French are rude, when actually the people they met were simply reacting to the abrasive nature of the tourist in their presence. People who are around you in the office, at the gym, in the street, or in your kitchen are constantly reacting to you. When you look at the expressions of those that you are talking to, you are looking at a "reflection" of yourself.

Remember the Funhouse at the carnival that had those crazy mirrors which distorted our reflection? Some made us look tall, short, fat, and skinny. Yet they were all a reflection of us. Similarly, everyone interprets us through their own set of values, judgments, beliefs, and perceptions. While there may be many interpretations, the one that is the most important is your partner's. Sometimes they may misinterpret you, but your response does not need to be harsh or critical. Regardless of your perception, it's worthwhile to try looking at yourself from their perspective.

Your partner's body language is a great mirror for you to look into. This is especially valuable when you look at your partner and see they're sad, disappointed, frustrated, or hurt as a result of your presence. In the previous example, although Adam escaped both attempts for change by his wife, if he was to look at her closely, he would have noticed that she seemed to retreat and close down. After years of eluding responsibility and not noticing her disappointment and frustration, Adam will probably wonder why she lost her passion and love for him.

Instead of always shifting the responsibility for everything to your partner, including their emotions and feelings, it's important to acknowledge the effect you have on them. You may be successful at convincing them you're right or they're wrong. Yet if you look close enough you will probably notice that you've wounded them in the process. *Can you see your own reflection by looking at your partner?*

If you want your relationship to not only last but to remain passionate and alive, when you notice that you've been a little ugly or closed to your partner's concerns or perspective, take immediate action to rectify the situation. Don't shift the entire responsibility for his/her emotions to your partner. Your partner is *influenced* by your actions.

Ultimately, we are all individually responsible for our own feelings, beliefs, attitudes, and actions. Don't take full responsibility for what others say, feel, or do. Yet if you are not experiencing the kind of connection with your partner that you'd like, don't put all of the blame on them either. Maybe you can adjust the way you are with them so that he/she may find it easier to react to you in the manner that you'd prefer.

If your partner is angry, afraid to open up, or insecure, you may want to reflect on why they are reacting to you in that manner. Is the way they are feeling or acting truly just the result of who they are, or is there anything that you say or do that has the one you love react this way? That's not always an easy question to answer, but certainly one worth asking from time to time.

Communicating And Shifting Attitudes

By being aware of what you're communicating you may change how you *feel* about a person or situation. When you stop and think about how you want to express yourself, many times you'll consider other factors that will shift how you're feeling.

Tony used to be quite agitated by his wife's habit of covering seemingly every square inch of the bathroom counter with her makeup, curlers, and accessories. Whenever he tried discussing the situation with Elizabeth, there was always a tone of disapproval and negativity in his voice.

After attending one of our seminars, Tony became much more aware of the way he talked to his partner, and began to try to eliminate the negativity from his comments and voice. It wasn't long before Tony noticed that as he consciously chose *how* to talk with Elizabeth about "the mess," he wouldn't be as bothered by it. By thinking and choosing how he would approach other situations as well, Tony noticed that the removal of the negativity left him feeling less upset and actually more able to find humor and a lightness more often.

Some people constantly criticize their partner. After learning more about communicating effectively they can *choose* to express themselves differently. Removing criticism, blame, or disapproval improves your chances of being listened to. But even more importantly, by expressing yourself in a more positive fashion, you will often end up feeling better about your partner as a result.

When you are in the criticizing mode, you don't communicate or feel a whole lot of warmth towards your partner. By reminding yourself that you love your partner, and your comments need to reflect that, you actually can feel more love and appreciation for them.

Instead of just venting or getting something off your chest, a more positive approach will leave you and your partner feeling more of a connection instead of distant and frustrated. The bottom line is that you can and will demonstrate that you do care about your relationship by consciously and effectively interacting with the one you love. Your change in approach and perspective is the beginning of a change in heart.

Being Genuine Instead Of Using Techniques

In the game of golf many little things need to be considered before each shot, such as distance, using the right club and holding it correctly, where one places their feet, keeping their head down, etc. Skills need to be learned to become a good golfer. The same is true in communication. You can learn the most important elements to include in your communications, as well as what to avoid. However, there is much to keep in mind. Like golf, it is easy to make mistakes.

Being effective communicators takes a lot of time, practice, and the knowledge that comes from making mistakes in order to become skilled. Give each other a break for the occasional blunders that you'll make, and strive together to reduce the frequency of misunderstandings between you.

Remember, what your lover really wants from you is genuine, sincere caring and thoughtfulness. If you give lip service to respecting him/her, but your tone of voice and facial expression give away the fact that you really don't feel that way, you could use this "technique" all day and get nowhere.

Communicating is not an issue of using techniques or saying what you're supposed to. If your partner hears your message but it looks, smells, or tastes like a "technique," it will be discarded as not being genuine and will have the opposite effect. People don't want their partner to use "techniques" on them. Obviously if your partner hears sincerity in your voice, he/she will be much more apt to respond in a positive fashion.

Tapping into the age-old lessons of being persuasive, creating greater understanding, and getting your messages clearly expressed to each other without creating conflict are important and essential endeavors for you to undertake. By doing so your partner and yourself will more regularly "hit the ball straight down the fairway instead of wandering through bramble bushes in the woods looking for lost balls." Congratulations on being committed enough to have read this far and for trying to develop more finesse and awareness.

The more you can trade places and honor each other's perspective, opinions, and approaches, the less conflict you will create. By standing in your partner's shoes and looking at yourself from their perspective once in a while, you will both begin to enjoy the benefits of a change of heart. In the next chapter you'll discover more ways to remove the negativity and increase the peace and love that you feel for each other.

~

CHAPTER 15

The Removal Of Disapproval
Remembering who you fell in love with

~

It's easy to forget about all of the positive attributes that you may love about your partner when encountering a part of their personality which is less endearing. Over the years, the possibility for this "temporary memory loss" increases as a couple learns more about each other and can more easily and often find perceived flaws that they never noticed or cared about when they first fell in love.

Unfortunately this tendency to focus on what you don't like can cast a shadow over the relationship like a big, dark rain cloud. When this occurs, it's essential that to find a way to instead focus on the good, on the positive and likable traits of your partner and spend less energy and time on those attributes that you don't like.

If you hear yourself repeatedly making negative comments, do your partner and yourself a favor by finding a way to bring the sunshine back to your life together. Keep in mind that there are many subtle and indirect ways of conveying negativity and a lack of respect, of which one of the most common is "giving advice."

Giving Advice

Although many times you may have learned lessons and have insights that can be of value to others, beware of giving *unsolicited* advice, especially to your partner. Your partner may be open to your advice if it is wanted and also given in a loving way. However, sharing your "wisdom" can be interpreted by the one you love that you think you are smarter or somehow superior to them.

Sometimes a friend may be quite open to your input or suggestions than your partner may be, but the nature of the relationship is quite different. For example, is a teenager more likely to want advice from their best friends or from their parents? Why do most teens resent parental advice? Primarily because they think their parents don't respect them as being intelligent enough to solve their own problems.

Couples who listen to each others' ideas and are open to their partners' suggestions usually convey respect and acknowledge that their partners could solve their problems on their own. On the other hand, couples who find their partners' approach "authoritative" interpret their "know it all" attitude as a lack of respect and confidence in them.

It takes practice to catch yourself before you launch into the advice mode. Once you are aware of your desire to "help" your partner solve his/her problem, ask if your opinion is wanted or for you to just listen. Resist your impulse to jump in with advice.

Women often complain that the men in their lives don't listen very well, and often try to "fix" their problems. Sometimes women may just want to talk things through rather than be told what to do. Talking out problems is a form of intimacy and connection for many women. Communicating helps them "relate" to and feel closer to their partner.

Since men are typically solution-oriented, this concept of just listening for the sake of listening can be confusing and frustrating at times. They may think, "Why are you telling me all of this if you don't want my opinions or don't want to find a solution to your problem?" Just listening to someone's problems without looking for answers is often thought of as impractical and a waste of time and energy by some men.

Without intending to insult his partner, a man may find himself giving unsolicited advice and thus upsetting the woman in his life. A woman might accuse her partner of not listening, while the man *knows* he was listening. After all, if he wasn't, how could he give advice?

After a hard day at the office, Natalie went home and began telling John all about it. John told her "You should quit that stupid job." She became upset and said he wasn't listening. He responded, "How can I not be listening? You said ......"

Natalie didn't mean John wasn't hearing her, she meant he was giving her advice instead of *just listening* to how frustrated she was with her job. She didn't want to quit, and wasn't sure she even wanted a solution. Natalie just wanted to talk with her partner and tell him how she was feeling. Since women also have a tendency to be indirect at times, this can leave men confused about what their partner really wants.

What seems clear to a woman may not be to a man. For example, "I just want you to support me in this" is unclear to a literal, matter-of-fact man who doesn't necessarily know what she means. He decides what he thinks she meant, proceeds accordingly, and may be wrong. Instead of just saying, "I want you to support me," a more clear request would be "I need your encouragement and support instead of your focus on potential flaws or weaknesses in my ideas."

Earlier Natalie said, "You're not listening." John took that very literally, and so of course he argued because he had heard every word. Natalie could have been more clear and said, "John, I know you care, mean well, and want to help. But I just want you to listen, not solve my problem for me. I just want to tell you about my day."

Naturally women want and deserve to be respected. Since they want to be thought of as capable of solving their own problems, they usually resent the suggestion that they aren't. Sometimes women want to share their experiences with their partners because it helps them to think through and clarify problems, while also helping them connect with the men in their lives.

On the other hand, most men are not as verbal and many like to temporarily forget about their problems. For example, men often want to leave behind the day's work when it is over, especially when it was a particularly rough day. Sometimes they just don't want to relive the details. They'd rather set aside the subject, and don't make a great effort to share their problems with their partner. Quite a few men are simply different in this manner.

Consider for a moment how most men interact on the phone. They are usually brief, and get right down to business. "What's going on? (Why did you call?) What are we going to do? When and where will we meet? O.K. Great. See you then. Good-bye." Yet many women will often talk for a while to the person they're going to meet in an hour. This just doesn't make sense to most men, whose approach is typically, "If you have more to say, save it and say it later when you get together."

Women often talk just for sole purpose of *relating*,
while the average man talks to *accomplish* something.

If you're a man and not sure if the woman in your life just wants you to listen or if she is looking for some advice or ideas about what to do, <u>ask</u>. It may *seem* as if she must be looking for advice or help, but that's not necessarily true. You will win more points if you resist being the Wizard of Oz with all the answers, and instead, just listen. This does not mean be patronizing or appear to be listening but actually mentally checked out. Not giving advice *doesn't mean having nothing to say.* Dialogue can and should be present when asked for. Occasionally, it's helpful to show you're really listening by asking questions.

When Natalie tells John that she's feeling overweight lately, John would do well by not telling her to start using the dormant exercise bike in their basement. Yet he might show he's listening by asking her a question such as, "Do you feel like that every day or just at certain times?" or "Why do you think you've been feeling that way?"

Many women do the very same thing that *they* resent by trying to help their man fix his problems. Even more so than most women, men are typically very independent and want to be seen as being capable of solving their own problems too. When women inject their advice and solutions without being asked, they will likely face some of the same reactions from their partner.

The difference is men, who *do want solutions*, often want to solve it on their own. They quite often don't talk about their problems, and figure they will be better off figuring out what to do in the privacy and quiet of their own mind.

Neither gender, therefore, likes to have their partner imply that they aren't smart enough to solve their own problems. Learning how not to subject your partner to your "wisdom" and advice may be much more difficult however. Most of us just don't realize when we are doing it.

Understanding that you each have a mutual desire to help will allow you to be more patient with each other. The next step is to clearly, and in a loving manner, communicate that you aren't looking for solutions, unless, in fact, you are. The more you listen and the less you preach and advise, the more respect your partner will feel; another simple but important step in the direction of maintaining the love and connection between you.

Doing It "Right"

If you want to keep your partner as a lover, as an active parent to your children, as a helper around the house, or even a partner in your business - it's important to not make them feel incompetent. After all, when you first met and fell in love, surely you didn't feel this person was inadequately equipped to go through life. Instead you were probably rather excited about sharing your life together.

Over time most things change, some of which are the result of our actions. A change in a couple's sex life is often related to comments over the years, but many don't see the connection. For example, I've had many people come to me and say, "My partner never wants to make love." Yet when I talk to their partners, there is usually no lack of interest in sex, but a lack of interest in having sex with their partner.

There are many, many possibilities of what could cause this loss of interest. Surprisingly one of the more common factors is that their partner has led them to believe they're boring or not very skilled in bed. They feel criticized, insulted, and have been corrected in an area which is very sensitive for most people.

Janet and Chris had been together for about three years when they came to see me. Chris complained that he had to constantly tell Janet what to do in bed, and she just *didn't get it.* He confided that she was "lost" when it came to sex. Even after he'd tell Janet what to do and what he liked, she wouldn't "do it right" and always seemed to forget what he'd told her. Chris said that sex was never their strong point as a couple, and now they rarely ever made love at all.

After talking with Janet, it was clear that Chris's comments and approach had left her feeling self-conscious and awkward in the area of sex. She told me that no matter what she tried, it was never right and she began to feel foolish and embarrassed when they were being sexual together. Janet missed having a sexual connection with a man, but had lost interest in making love with Chris. Over the years she decided that Chris was the one with the problem, and secretly she fantasized about being with a man who wouldn't be so particular and hard to please.

When a person has been told enough times that they are incompetent, they might eventually say to themselves, "Why should I even bother trying?" If you want to encourage "change" in your partner, the way you express yourself can help you get what you want. What you communicate plays a major role in the final results.

The following phrases are typical of how Kelly used to talk to Brett: "Honey, that's not how you hold a child, give her here, let me show you! What a typical man! Come here. Oh, yes, mommy will take care of you. Daddy just doesn't understand."

It's irrelevant whether you're talking to your partner about how to make love with you, how to change diapers, how to discipline the children, or how to wash the dishes. Be careful not to approach the situation as if they have no idea what they're doing, or you will get the opposite reaction of what you really want. If a woman repeatedly tells her husband that he is clueless in helping with their baby, she'll soon be doing it all, and then complaining that she doesn't get enough help.

After Kelly went to one of our seminars, she realized that she had been telling Brett that he was incompetent quite often. She committed to becoming more patient and helping him learn, and is now more gentle and careful in her approach. Kelly knows that if she doesn't imply that Brett is inadequate, he'll want to learn and be more eager to help. It's taken a little time and effort, but Kelly has grown in her ability to communicate more effectively. Now she's more likely to say:

"It's taking a while to get comfortable holding her, isn't it, Honey? It took me a while too. Let me show you what seems to work well. Just try holding her like this. Yes, that's great! You'll be an old pro before you know it! You're a great dad."

As you can probably tell from many of the examples used, quite a few women often complain that their partners don't help around the house enough. Again one of the most common reasons is the "incompetence" factor. This used to be true for Kelly and Brett as well. Brett used to help with tasks such as doing the dishes, but he never did them "right." Here is how Kelly used to approach him:

"Brett, you wash dishes like a guy. Look, there's still food on this plate! It's really not that hard to do it right!" It isn't difficult to see why Brett didn't help out very often. Now Kelly has changed her approach, and is more apt to say, "Thanks so much for doing the dishes! I really didn't feel like doing them tonight." She knows that she doesn't always have to point out deficiencies and the dishes don't have to be perfect everytime. If she sees an ongoing problem, she might add, gently and in a loving manner, "You might want to be more careful with some of the plates. I noticed a little food was still on a couple of them. But really, it's no big deal. Thanks so much for helping."

It may be frustrating at times when your partner doesn't exhibit a proficiency at something that seems easy or obvious to you. Try to be patient and approach the situation with care. Whether it's paying the bills, programming the VCR, driving, disciplining the children, cooking, playing tennis, making love, or whatever the endeavor may be, implying your partner is "incompetent" can quickly stunt their interest and also create resentment between you.

Most people don't recognize when they are being critical. They don't feel the suggestion of incompetence that they are sending to their partner. It may take a little practice and making a few mistakes before you are able to eliminate the negativity and criticism from your comments. If you catch yourself implying incompetence, simply apologize and restate what you want in a more loving manner. It *will* make a difference, and your partner will appreciate your effort and feel more respected.

If you are the recipient of these "incompetence" messages, *you* will know, even if your partner doesn't, what was just said. It's important to express how you experienced their message. Remember to do so in a way that doesn't accuse them of being *an incompetent communicator.* For example, Brett could say:

"You really are unbelievable. Do you know what you just said! You made me feel like a jerk for not knowing how to hold our baby! Someday I hope you'll get a clue how to communicate!" Instead, Chris is better off by saying, "I'm sure you didn't mean to hurt my feelings. Yet when you talk to me that way, I feel like I'm being told I have no idea what I'm doing. Sometimes it seems I can't ever do anything right for you. I don't want to feel that way, and I know that's not your intention. I just need you to be a little more helpful and patient with me."

It may take a little more thought, effort, or time to remove the suggestion of incompetence, but the response you receive will be directly tied to how you express yourself!

You Are Good Enough! (And People Like You)

Throughout our lives we have heard many messages from our parents, teachers, coaches, and friends that suggested we simply "weren't good enough." We didn't study hard enough, try hard enough, or maybe didn't care enough. We could have done better or weren't living up to our potential. This is not quite the same as being "incompetent," yet creates many of the same problems.

Most of us receive our share of this discouraging form of "encouragement." Often the comments are made with the best intentions. Usually someone who cares about us is simply trying to spur us on towards becoming even better. Yet both you and your partner have probably heard plenty of these messages in your life already. The last person you want telling you that you're not good enough is your lover, your friend, your partner. You both will benefit by avoiding these subtle messages of disapproval and putting more energy into striving to accept and love your partner as they are.

Joan and Al were both in their early 50's, and had met five years earlier at a singles dance for divorcees. Tentative regarding marriage, they decided to live together for a while first. During this period they began to experience some frustration with each other. Because they truly wanted the relationship to work, they attended a *"Keeping Love Alive"* seminar to smooth out the "bumps in the road." During a dinner break they shared the following stories with me:

> One afternoon Al returned home from work and was quite tired. Going inside, Al saw the unfolded laundry on the couch and newspapers spread out on the coffee table and floor. "The house is really a mess," Al said when he saw Joan. But Joan heard, *"You haven't been doing enough around here!"* He continued, "By the way, have you finished fixing up the guest room yet?" Joan's temperature was rising. She inhaled deeply as she heard, *"I bet you were too lazy to finish the guest room too!"*

Joan *interpreted* his statements as implying she wasn't pulling her weight because of Al's facial expressions and tone of voice. Joan had been feeling increasingly criticized by Al, and so his statements resulted in more anger and hurt between the two of them. Joan was poised for a swift counterattack by this time. She especially resented the notion that she was lazy. As a result of her building frustration, Joan's rebuttal was sharp and hostile.

Any of these comments could have been no problem for some couples. Sometimes we may be especially sensitive to being criticized, thus misinterpreting our partner's comments as attacks. At other times, regardless of the words used, the facial expressions and gestures alone suggest that our partner is disapproving of us and we're not living up to their expectations.

On another day, Joan asked Al if he would take her grandchildren to the park. Al agreed and piled the kids in the car. While there, her granddaughter, Suzy, fell and scraped her knee. When they returned home, Joan saw the scrape and glared at Al. Then she said, "Why does something like this always happen when you are watching the kids?" She proceeded to clean and bandage Suzy's knee. Al felt resentful because of her suggestion that he wasn't a very good grandparent, and that once again he wasn't good enough for her.

These scenarios may seem insignificant. But they represent more than just isolated incidents of poor communication. The messages Joan and Al sent to each other each cut deeply into their feelings of being loved, admired, and respected. With years of this type of communication between two people, the resentment can build and the tendency to tune-out one's partner increases.

Al and Joan were on vacation. Joan was responsible for navigating since she had the map and Al was driving. They were driving along while talking about their vacations as youngsters when Al saw a sign that made him wonder if they had missed a turn. He asked Joan to find where they were on the map, and sure enough, they had missed their exit a half an hour earlier.

Al hated going out of his way, and they had to drive another half hour just to get back to the turn they missed. His jaw was clenched and he wasn't talking, and instead just stared straight ahead as he drove. Finally, he looked over at Joan and said, "Can't you ever pay attention to the map! This always happens. Now because you can't talk and read a map at the same time, we've wasted over an hour!"

Al never used the words, "You're not good enough," but that's exactly what he told her. Joan felt hurt and insulted; she had simply a made an honest mistake. Al could have said, "I hate missing my turn and going so far out of the way. I guess we both weren't paying attention. I probably should have asked you where we were supposed to turn and had you help me watch for the exit. I know it wasn't your fault." But he didn't, and sometimes you won't either.

Sometimes people just react. But when you do this, you can usually see by the look on your partner's face that you just told them they weren't good enough. Just go back and apologize. Al said, "I'm sorry Joan. That wasn't very fair. It's both of our jobs to watch where we're going. I didn't mean to hurt your feelings. You know how I am about wasting time. Let's both try to be more alert. I'm sorry, Honey."

Make the effort to heal the wound when you catch yourself accusing your partner of not being good enough. Otherwise you will have created a little more tension, separation, and distance between you and the one you love.

Be careful not to convey indirect messages of disapproval and how you see that your partner isn't good enough. Those messages may make your partner feel more and more unloved, unappreciated, and disrespected. Since many people already don't feel like they're good enough, whether in their careers, as parents, or as partners, they may be especially sensitive to reinforcement of that fear.

Communicate what you need and want in a manner that is neutral and as pleasant as possible - yet direct. If your partner doesn't do the best job washing the dishes, fixing the fence, washing clothes, or making dinner, don't point out their poor job. Focus on what they did right and acknowledge their effort.

The removal of disapproval is essential as you strive to be the partner you aspire to be. Focus on what you love about them instead of how they could be closer to your ideal of perfect. Remember that this person is the same person you fell in love with, and choose to be more patient, forgiving, and appreciative.

~

~

*"The deepest principle in human nature
is the craving to be appreciated."*
William James

~

Chapter 16

Power Tools

Practical ways of getting through to your partner

~

Analogies

Sometimes you can clearly and directly express your feelings, needs, desires, concerns, or expectations, and yet your message seems to go in one ear and out the other. With a little thought and a good analogy, many times you can "get through" to your partner in a manner that has them truly understand what you're saying.

Analogies are simply unrelated stories that illustrate a point. By telling a story, you can help your partner feel and visualize what you're talking about. Your partner will become involved with the story, while also looking for how it relates to the immediate conversation. Analogies are somewhat of a puzzle for the brain.

Some people believe they are poor story tellers, or that they aren't good at "drawing analogies." It's not as difficult as one might think, yet a little practice certainly makes this approach to communication become easier and more natural.

Today most people rarely utilize this approach in their attempts to communicate. However, Native Americans used analogies and stories as their principle means of teaching when books were not yet a part of their culture. Even Jesus often spoke in "parables" to make his points understandable and more memorable. Psychologists and authors have occasionally "packaged" this timeless style of communication by giving it a variety of names, such as Gary Smalley's "Emotional Word Pictures." Yet regardless of what you call analogies, they are a very effective way of getting your message across.

When using an analogy, it's essential that your story makes sense and leaves the listener with a clear meaning or it will be ineffective. When you become more skilled in the area of telling analogies, you can find ways to include more emotion and feeling into them so they will have even more impact.

You may not always be able to spontaneously formulate great analogies in the middle of a conversation or in the heat of a conflict. But for the times when you know you want to express something important to your partner and you have the opportunity to think things through beforehand, analogies can be a very handy tool.

> Matt and Dianne had been together for fifteen years, and had very little conflict in their relationship. Unfortunately they did not share much passion either, and over the years Dianne became increasingly frustrated with the lack of intimacy between them. She felt as if she was constantly giving love and affection to Matt, but he rarely reciprocated. After being encouraged to use an analogy to express how she felt to Matt, Dianne said to him:

> "Matt, have you ever hugged someone but that person didn't hug you back? They stood there with their arms limp at their sides, and simply *let you hug them*, as if they were enduring it just so they wouldn't appear rude?"

> Matt acknowledged that he had such an experience, and he remembered feeling awkward and uncomfortable afterwards. Dianne continued, "Sometimes that's how I feel at the end of the day when you come home. I've been looking forward to seeing you, but you're often grumpy or tired and don't want to talk. I look forward to spending the weekends together, but most of the time you want to be alone or do things by yourself. When I want to be intimate you occasionally "go along" but rarely initiate on your own. I need to feel more loved by you."

Dianne's analogy was simple and short, but it did give a clear example of how she felt in a variety of situations with her husband. This approach is far more effective than just saying, "I hate it you come home and you just want to be alone or the first thing you say to me is critical or negative." This type of statement is often met with resistance, defensiveness, blame, or denial.

For analogies, it is best to use a situation that is unrelated to your circumstances, but which would leave a person feeling like you do. Your partner will be more likely to caught up in the story long enough to get the message. In a direct approach regarding a very sensitive topic, often the listener's guard comes up at the first indication of what you're going to say. The analogy sometimes suspends the tendency to defend or counterattack long enough for you to get your point across.

There is no magic formula for the optimal length of an analogy, yet it is important to keep it brief. If you get too wordy or too elaborate, you may lose your partner's attention or patience. When you can create an analogy in advance, try to make it short and simple. Your story will be even more effective if it pertains to a subject that is important and interesting to your partner. Tailor it to them personally. What do they relate to, what do they care about? To illustrate this, let's use another example from Dianne. One of Matt's greatest passions is hunting, for which he has many guns.

"Honey, remember that Winchester rifle you got from your best friend before we were married? You always took it with you hunting, spent hours cleaning it, and were always sighting it in. It was your favorite and clearly one of your most prized possessions. Over the years you've accumulated many newer and more expensive guns and now that old one just collects a lot of dust and never gets used.

Obviously guns don't have feelings, but if they did that Winchester would probably be lonely and feel left out. That's how I feel. Once I was the most important thing to you, and you used to spend a lot of energy on me, on us. I really felt I mattered to you. Now I feel like I'm not as interesting to you and you've moved on to other things. I really want to feel that special, that important to someone, and I want that someone to be *you*."

Dianne's analogy was perfect for Matt but would be inappropriate for someone else. Look for ways to relate your story to the individual and specific interests of your partner whenever possible. Another example from this couple's life will further illustrate this point. Knowing that Dianne was very much an animal lover, Matt decided to use an analogy that would include their new puppy, Ruggles. Matt had been trying to help Dianne out more around the house, but it seemed she always picked apart whatever he did and it was beginning to really irritate him. Here's what Matt said to illustrate his point:

> "Dianne, imagine for a moment that you were trying to train Ruggles to jump to get a treat in your hand. Ruggles jumps, but not high enough to get the treat. Not only doesn't he get the treat, but then he gets scolded and hit with a newspaper! After a few times of not doing it right and then getting punished, he doesn't want to try anymore. That's how I feel when I try to help you around the house. It doesn't matter if it's the dishes, vacuuming, or laundry, whatever I try to help with you find fault in what I've done and it's killing my interest quickly."

Obviously you don't need to use analogies for every situation. Use analogies sparingly and in moderation. If you constantly talk in stories, this will become annoying and ineffective because your partner will stop listening at the onset of "another analogy." Straight forward, old-fashioned direct communication will often suffice. But when the issue is very sensitive or after repeated attempts to have your partner understand how you feel have failed, a carefully crafted analogy can be quite helpful.

Reframing

Another useful tool to use that can improve the possibility you will be listened to and understood is called "reframing." This approach also "opens the door," allowing your partner to more easily hear your message. If your message has any negative implications, it's a good possibility that your partner may "tune out" what you have to say. Reframing also reduces the chance that your partner will become defensive, improving your chances of being understood and having some impact.

Ying and Yang, hard and soft, dark and light, there is always an opposite or a reverse angle to things in life. Just like every coin has a head & a tail, most negative personality traits have a positive side. Almost all frustrating behaviors are a positive attribute taking a negative form. By understanding and recognizing this, you can often find a way to get a different perspective on situations around you, allowing you to communicate about them differently as well. Through this change of heart or perspective you are more able to state your case in such a manner that your partner won't shut you out because he/she won't feel attacked.

Think of what is frustrating about your partner.
What is a positive aspect of that same behavior?

Let's say, in your opinion, your partner is stubborn. You want them to listen to you, but they are defiant and will not. Telling him/her they are "stubborn" will probably not be well received, and your comments may simply be ignored. Because you are frustrated by how stubborn they can be, *disapproval* comes through in your voice. You want your partner to listen more and to consider your perspective, but you're not sure how to accomplish this.

Ask yourself "What is the *positive* side of stubbornness?" A stubborn person is typically persistent, determined, able to resist peer pressure, and holds strong convictions. In your particular situation, these same characteristics are frustrating you. This doesn't mean your partner is broken and needs to be fixed or has a problem. Yet there is a way to become more "user friendly," which would be valuable in your mutual pursuit to have a satisfying long-term relationship together.

Your approach shifts when you focus on the opposite side of the coin - your partner's *strengths.* Instead of opening the conversation with their "weakness" as you see it, try beginning with acknowledging your partner by expressing what you appreciate and respect about them. From there you can eventually mention how that strength can be a limitation. Not only is your approach easier to listen to, but in the process it also changes the way you look at and feel about your partner.

Let's return to the hypothetical example of your stubborn partner. After looking for the positive side of this negative attribute, you no longer *only* see "stubbornness." Now you also see a person who isn't a push-over, isn't wishy-washy, isn't spineless. This incorporates a tone or respect in your voice, leading you to feel better about them at the same time.

After you've acknowledged your partner for being strong, determined, and someone who isn't afraid to take a stand, you would then mention how sometimes that strength is frustrating to you because they rarely will consider your perspective!!

You can be heard more easily because you haven't come out with guns blazing. Instead you've demonstrated through your words and tone of voice that you actually respect and appreciate your partner. With this more palatable approach, he/she can often admit to limitations and be more willing to consider trying to change.

Don't begin your approach to your partner expressing what you don't like about them as this closes the door to their listening any further.

Finding the positive side of some behaviors "on the spot" can occasionally be difficult. Again this tool is often the most useful when you have the chance to think about what you want to say prior to your actual conversation. No approach can guarantee success, yet the better you get at using tools such as analogies and reframing, the more possibility you have of achieving the results that you would like

Other one-word examples of reframing how you may see your partner are as follows:

Perceived Limitation	Related Positive Attribute
Idealistic	Optimistic
Excitable	Enthusiastic
Perfectionist	Organized, Orderly
Nosy	Curious, Inquisitive
Manipulative	Persuasive
Reckless	Courageous
Blunt	Direct, Straightforward
Impulsive	Spontaneous
Slow-Paced	Systematic, Methodical
Impatient	Action-Oriented

Instead of telling your partner they're impatient, try expressing how you respect the fact that he/she takes action and gets things done, yet sometimes it would be appreciated if they were a little more patient.

In the process of reframing what you see as your partner's limitations, if he/she can hear you're being genuine, the two of you will have a much more civilized discussion. You also naturally convey more warmth and love when you can articulate what you appreciate and respect about your partner, improving their receptivity to your message.

Many times you'll find that some of your partner's weaknesses are simply the less-than-desirable side of their greatest strengths.

For example, a person who is very direct and straightforward is also often blunt and abrasive. Someone who is highly motivated can also be a workaholic.

Think about the people you have dated or were married to and recall what you were attracted to and what ended up splitting you apart. Many times it's the same thing. A great majority of divorced people will tell you that what they found the most attractive about their previous partner was what also ended up driving them apart.

A man at one of our seminars told me that he loved how agreeable and easy-going his first wife was when he met her. After their marriage she rarely stood up for herself and became passive and over-accommodating to him. Another example was a woman who respected her "partner to be" when she first met him because he didn't care about money and wasn't materialistic. Unfortunately, that led to unwise expenditures, bills left unpaid, and no aspirations.

There are times when it is important to not only talk about problem areas, but to be able to *get through* to your partner in order to see results. *Attacking* will serve only shut you out and making your partner defensive. Instead, identify the positive side of what you perceive as their limitation, acknowledge him/her for it, and then tell your partner your concerns in a manner that shows you still respect, appreciate, and love them.

This is one of the most simple but effective ways to improve your chances of getting through to your partner when you have important concerns or requests.

The Art Of Making Requests

Whenever you need your partner to change, help, or respond in any manner, don't use begging, pleading, whining, blackmail, or guilt. Instead look for ways to turn your comments into requests. You'll find that pleasant yet firm requests that are direct and without anger or disapproval will be much more successful.

Regardless of what you may be concerned about, whether it is the way your partner talks to you, makes love to you, or cleans the bathroom, making requests rather than demands will dramatically improve your chances of achieving the desired end result. When you approach issues by making demands, your commands will meet resistance, impairing your pursuit of whatever action may need to be taken or agreements/ understandings that may need to be reached.

In your relationship with your partner, approach with a request.
This makes it much easier for them to hear you and to also
be willing to respond accordingly.

Never use a sarcastic, "parental," or authoritative tone with your partner while making the request. It is helpful to allow them to see that you are serious and firm about the request, but that it is not a command. If you said, "You *have to* call me if you're going to be late!" you would be making a command. Your partner's response could then be, "Really? What are you going to do, send me to my room?!" Even if what your asking for makes sense and seems reasonable, rephrasing your comment into the form of a request helps your partner hear you more clearly and leaves them without a feeling of rebelliousness or anger.

A more palatable approach would be, "I know it doesn't always seem necessary for to you to call me when you're going to be late, and I probably shouldn't worry. But would you do me a favor anyway and try to make more of an effort to call when you think you might be late? I would really appreciate it." It's much easier to want to respond to this request when phrased this way. You're acknowledging that your partner does have a choice, and can "do you a favor" by honoring your request, rather than simply *obeying* your command.

If you make a request and your partner follows through, he/she gets to be the "hero." Instead of being forced to do something and complying, a choice is made to do so under their own free will, which makes your partner feel better about him/herself and you. The following example will illustrate this further:

Mary said to her husband, Jim, "It's very important that invitations get sent out to all of Billy's friends for his birthday party. Since I'll be out of town on business, you'll have to do it." The task was given to Jim and now he "must" do it. If he doesn't, she'll be disappointed and angry with him upon her return. Jim is already quite busy & now resents having to do it.

It would be better for everyone if Jim didn't resent being given the job. He would take on the project with more enthusiasm and no resentment if he could be the "hero" by volunteering to help his wife, making it a favor to her rather than the fulfillment of an obligation. If Mary would have simply made a pleasant request, chances are he would have willingly complied. Here is Mary's approach in the form of a request:

"Jim, Billy's birthday snuck up on me and I haven't had time to send any invitations to his friends for his upcoming party. I'm going to be out of town on business for the next few days and I won't be able to get to it. Is there any way you could help me out and take care of it?" If Jim says yes, which he probably will, he is now "doing her a favor" and gets to be the nice guy. She thanks him for it and he's much happier to help.

We all have different priorities. For example, to one person yard work may not be important, while it may be much more so to their partner. Jim and Mary have a very large yard, and Jim has been working a lot and has a hard time doing everything to keep the yard under control. Instead of demanding that Mary help him, especially because she's not passionate about the yard, Jim would be better off making a request.

"Mary, I know you're not that concerned about the yard being immaculate like I am. But it's been hard to find enough time to keep on top of it, and I was wondering if you'd be willing to help me out once a week by just spending about an hour or so by watering the flower garden and the lawn?"

Jim could have said, "You *have to* help me deal with this yard!" But instead, if Jim makes his *request* reasonable and doesn't imply that Mary is lazy, she'll be much more willing to make an effort to help. The same principles apply when making requests for change in areas other than chores and household projects. For instance, if you wanted your partner to be less passive in the bedroom or to be more patient with you, a request could be made that encourages a positive response.

Mary would like Jim to be more imaginative and energetic in the bedroom. They have fallen into the "missionary position" rut and Mary wants their sex life to be more interesting and include some foreplay for a change. Her words could imply that he's been pretty boring or lazy. Mary could even demand that he change by saying:

"Look Jim, if you can't show more effort by mixing things up once in a while or doing a little foreplay before we have intercourse, I'm not going to have sex with you anymore. I don't feel like you're making love. Instead it seems like you're just going through the motions to have an orgasm, and I feel used!"

Jim may reluctantly or sheepishly comply, but Mary's comments stand a greater chance of creating defensiveness and resistance. Instead, he could earn appreciation from Mary for responding to her "request" because he wanted to, out of his love for her and commitment to their relationship. This would more likely be accomplished if Mary approached Jim in a manner more like this:

"Jim, I know we've been married quite a while now, and the passion and intensity isn't always going to be like it was when we first met. I know we still love each other. Yet sometimes I feel like we're just going through the motions when we have sex. We rely a lot on the 'missionary position,' and I especially miss the foreplay before intercourse. I think we both could make more of an effort to put in more energy and be a little more creative. I'm certainly willing to try. Will you?"

Mary has made a request, not a demand, and opened the door for Jim to share his feelings about it. Just as importantly, Mary has taken responsibility for her part instead of putting all the blame on him, which makes it much easier for Jim to accept partial responsibility himself. As a side note, asking for your partner to talk with you shouldn't be a request that can't be honored. A question of when and for *how long* may actually be an issue though. Your partner should never reject your request to talk out problems. Doing so is a sign of someone with too much "control" in the relationship.

Be careful to not make a request that sounds more like a demand by your tone of voice and accompanying facial and non-verbal messages that signal disapproval. Try to keep your requests neutral and without any message of negativity. And always leave your partner room to choose to honor your request, making them the "hero" instead of the one who is simply "doing their duty."

A lot of people ask, "How can I get my partner to listen to me?" The way you approach your partner can "open the door" to their receptivity, such as using analogies, reframing, and making requests as discussed above.

Finally, people usually listen to people who listen to them. Many people are totally unaware that they often don't listen to their partner, which is why their partner doesn't listen to them. Remember, your ability to communicate with each other effectively will carry you through the challenges of life together as a team, helping you make the necessary adjustments along the way. You can stand the test of time with your pride, love, and respect intact.

~

~

"We are built to conquer environment, solve problems, achieve goals, and we find no real satisfaction or happiness in life without obstacles to conquer and goals to achieve."
Maxwell Maltz

~

CHAPTER 17

Dynamic Duo

The distinction between sex and intimacy & what men and women want

~

Up until the late 1900's, sex was simply a means to an end for many in America. Some religious doctrines suggested that sex was for the sole purpose of producing children. The idea of people having sex for pleasure was certainly not embraced by society or many churches. Now it seems that the pendulum has swung so far in the opposite direction that for many the purpose of sex is primarily just for *pleasure*.

Because we are saturated with images of sex through television, magazines, and movies, we probably think about it much more often than most people did in the 1940's or 50's. While an argument could be built that sex is over-rated or inflated in its importance, there is no doubt that it is of great interest and sometimes concern to couples in the 90's.

Sex is the one thing we reserve exclusively for our partner, making it the most defining distinction between a friendship and a relationship. While it is quite possible to exist without it, most people would prefer to share a passionate and regular sex life with their partner. Aside from the obvious physical pleasure sex can bring, it can also be the vehicle for sharing emotional intimacy with our partner.

We all need to give love and feel loved to some degree, for which most of us turn to sex. Instead of focusing on how to increase your "sexual pleasure" through techniques, this book will look at how your sex life can be more fulfilling, satisfying, and passionate, and the important role that intimacy plays.

The Distinction Between Sex & Intimacy

"Intimacy" describes the expression and feeling of love and affection between two people. It can take many shapes and forms, such as a hug, a long walk together, a thoughtful gift, lending of a helpful hand, showing forgiveness, or a gentle caress.

When you tell your partner why you love them, appreciate them, and enjoy being together, that is *intimacy*. When a couple holds hands as their plane takes off, or cuddles up next to each other before going to sleep, that is intimacy. When one person does something romantic for their partner, that is intimacy.

Sex and intimacy are related but distinctly different. Because making love with one's partner is a form of intimacy, some people mistakenly condense the two terms as being one in the same. And while they are both important, one without the other usually results in at least one partner, if not both, feeling unfulfilled. Some couples are sweet and affectionate but rarely have sex, and others have sex but share little or no affection and intimacy outside of the bedroom. Even intercourse can be accomplished without an exchange of much intimacy because of a lack of passion or affection.

> Jeff and Lisa are in bed "making love." He prefers to be on his back, and relies on Lisa to make most of the effort. Midway through the experience Lisa notices that Jeff's eyes are closed and his hands and arms are limp at his sides. She says nothing, but can't help but feel that Jeff isn't really excited about making love or being with her at the moment.
>
> To Lisa it doesn't feel very personal, as if he's expressing his love to her. He doesn't seem present, and she feels a little sad afterwards as she lies next to him. For her, the experience wasn't very fulfilling because instead of a passionate exchange of love making, it was routine and unemotional.

What Women Want

When referring to the complex area of sex, making blanket statements such as "Men want ..... and women want ....." is difficult to do because it overly simplifies an extremely personal and individualistic issue. Clearly there are a wide variety of different kinds of sexual relationships and experiences that people can share and enjoy.

To be more precise, what men and women each want in the area of sex needs to be defined on an individual basis. Thus, whatever a person is missing or longs for in regards to the subject of sex is simply what that person needs at that time in their life. For example, some women enjoy having a lot of tenderness and affection but crave a little "intensity" in the bedroom. Other women may experience their share of intense, physical sex but desire more affection, consideration, and gentleness for balance.

Yet when looking at the population as a whole and talking with a great number of people, some conclusions can be drawn based upon the majority. *Over the years what women have told me they want spans quite a diverse range. Yet the majority of women have told me that they want more intimacy in their relationships.*

Women want to feel connected with their partner and genuinely loved. They usually want to be told why their man loves them, and what is it about her that he recognizes as special. Women have often said they want to be held more, kissed more, caressed more, touched intimately more, and talked to more. If they were to have more sex, they want it to be more "passionate" love-making. They want more intimacy *in and out* of the bedroom.

Women also need to be acknowledged for what they contribute to the family and their man's life. They need to be respected as intelligent and capable, and appreciated for all of their wonderful attributes and special features. The average women wants more hugs, more affection, more intimacy regularly. A woman often wants to be told they are beautiful, that their partner wants to be with her and enjoys being together.

Often men can get along without reinforcement and intimacy for long periods of time, and so they assume the same is true for women. Unfortunately quite a few men still think they can sustain a woman with occasional bursts of intimacy, such as a nice gift, or a rare verbal acknowledgment.

Most women need and want more than just sporadic maintenance intimacy. They need daily attention to keep them running smoothly and happily. After couples marry, many men only put forth the effort to show what they think is the necessary amount of "romance." They often base their conclusions on how much *they* need, and then give just a little more.

> *It's not the flowers, chocolates, poems,*
> *or gifts that women really want.*
> *What they really want are the gestures*
> *that show that their partner loves them and*
> *cares enough to expend some energy showing it!*

Women typically expect and appreciate having much more involvement from their relationships. They usually want more consistent and enthusiastic expressions of love and affection. They want to know, regularly, that they aren't being taken for granted.

> *Many marriages eventually end because men*
> *never really take their partner's needs seriously.*

Many of the married women who I've talked that have had extra-marital affairs said they fell for men who were interested in them, who talked with and listened to them. The men they were drawn to were enthused about them and showed it. The feelings of respect, appreciation, and passion were missing in their marriage. It is my belief that missing those feelings of intimacy has led more women to having affairs than a mere sexual attraction.

Women who have high self-esteem and believe in equality aren't satisfied with just being a sexual object. They want to be seen as much more than that, and rightfully resent some men's attempts to have them be just a "sex toy." Many women resent a man's interest in having uninvolved sex, and expect more from their partner than "just sex."

Most women aren't satisfied if the physical sex is *all* they have. Even if they regularly experience orgasms, most women will get bored if that's all their sex life consists of. They must feel love and connection with their partner as well. While this may not be news to women, quite a few men either don't know this or don't really take it seriously.

For many women, even though they may enjoy orgasms and the physical sensations, sex is more of a vehicle for "making love" and sharing affection and intimacy with their partner. Since women often say they need to feel more loved, if they did, they may feel more inclined to have more sex, which is what many men would like.

Thankfully, an increasing number of women today feel free to take more initiative and allow themselves to experience sex for pleasure and intimacy. Today more women are able to ask for more of what they want and need from their partner. Successful relationships usually include a man who respects this quality in his female counterpart.

What Men Want

Men often say they wish that relationships were "easier." Working at a relationship seems like just that, more "work." Their expectations are different as a group, and they often would like being in a relationship to mean more fun. Since men can often survive on less "intimacy" than their female counterparts, they crave more of the pleasure and enjoyment that sex brings them. Thus it makes sense that quite a large number of men report that they'd like to have *more sex.*

Yet men don't just want more sex if it will end up being boring. Many men feel their partner is passive sexually. If men have to convince their partner to make love, or she appears apathetic about it, sex loses much of its appeal. Women may crave passion, but so do men. Yet men often aren't as concerned about the experience being an exchange of love as they are excited by a woman's sexual intensity and assertiveness.

What men want more of in the arena of sex and intimacy is very diverse and individual. Yet what I hear the most often from men is their partner is not assertive enough sexually. Since this is something obviously quite a few men desire but don't experience, to them it is intriguing. Men often fantasize about a woman who loves sex and would love to have sex with him, and being with a woman who knows what she likes and is assertive about experiencing sexual pleasure.

That explains why a sensual or sexy woman captures the interest of so many men compared to the average woman who does not exude any sexual energy. Why are so many men attracted to women who wear mini-skirts, sheer blouses, tight leather pants, or low-cut tops? Because men interpret a woman's choice of this type of clothing as a sign that she likes to be sensual and sexual. While this may or not be true, they imagine that she's probably very sexual by nature. Even if her body is comparable to another woman, some men believe that her attitude would probably make her a lot more fun. While this is certainly not always accurate, it's simply an assumption that many men make.

The majority of men I've talked to say the woman in their life is either shy, reserved, waits for direction, or let's him make love *to* her. Men don't want to make love *to* their partner, they want it to be more of an exchange. Sometimes women just focus on their partner's pleasure, afraid to do whatever feels good to *her*. If you are the man and you wish your partner was more outgoing sexually - then it's time to speak up! Don't make your partner wrong for the way she's been in the past - just mention that you'd like to try something new, and what that would be.

If you are a woman who has been a little shy intimately, simply tell your man that you'd like to try being more assertive. Many men would appreciate the fact that their partner felt so safe, comfortable, and aroused that she was assertively passionate, and experiencing great pleasure, as a result of being with him. To be fair, *both* partners can usually become much more involved and assertive.

Sometimes women say they are afraid to do what they want because it will "make them look too experienced."

Instead of worrying about what your partner might think, couples would do well to talk about what they each would like more and less of, which we'll discuss more in the upcoming chapters. Lovemaking can be very much like dancing with someone. There can be more of a synchronicity with an appreciation of each other's interests and needs. With this kind of a spirit, you don't step on each other's toes, and instead find a rhythm that works for both of you.

Some couples become stuck in the rut of, "I don't want to give you what you want because I'm not getting what I want." I know men who resent their wife's lack of interest or willingness to be sexual with them. I also know women who are not interested in being sexual with their husband because they aren't intimate enough and the desire just isn't there as a result. Sometimes these people are married to each other, and the solution seems clear enough to everyone except for the couple who's in the middle of it!

Whatever it is that you or your partner want in regards to your sexual relationship is really what counts, not what other couples or the majority want. By communicating *your* interests and desires, the two of you can begin making more of an effort to make sure both of your needs are taken care of.

Couples will benefit when both partners see each others needs as valid and important. Regardless of which partner you are and whether you want more sex, more intimacy, or both; as a couple you should both be able to have what you each want and desire. Take your partner's interests seriously. Remember that sex and intimacy are in fact different even though they can be related. One does not replace the other, and both are just as important to keeping the passion alive in your relationship.

~

~

"What is most beautiful in virile men is something feminine; what is most beautiful in feminine women is something masculine."
Susan Sontag

~

CHAPTER 18

The Heart Of The Matter

Why interest fades & getting the desire back

~

There are a multitude of reasons why couples can experience a decline in their sex lives. Distractions may have kept them pre-occupied, such as the loss of a good job, prolonged illness, death of one's parent, or maybe building a new home. Couples may also have a hard time maintaining active sex lives because of frequent travel, exhaustion, depression, insecurities, or the pressures of children. Dealing with any one of these situations, which is only to name a few of the possibilities, is a complex subject in itself.

Regardless of the situation that created a loss of desire for sex, a couple must acknowledge the value and importance of a healthy sex life and find a way to get back on track. This intimate connection is vital to the longevity of a passionate relationship as it is one of the most important emotional bridges between two partners.

You can exist without sex. But a relationship based on affection, respect, intimacy, and a profound appreciation and love for each other is stronger and obviously more exciting.

Having a solid sexual relationship with your partner
can help you stay connected emotionally,
and dramatically improves your chances of long-term success.

One of the most prevalent sources of a diminished sex life is simply the couple isn't very "in love" outside of the bedroom in their day to day life together. Unresolved conflicts, resentments, or frustration between two people over an extended period of time usually lead to a loss of interest in being intimate and sexual with each other.

It's not uncommon for couples to tell me their relationship is fine except for their sex life. What they don't usually understand is that their lack of a sex life is directly related to the rest of their relationship. That's why a sexy night gown or movie isn't enough to add much of a lasting spark. The underlying feelings and attitudes that a couple has towards sex and each other are what needs to be examined.

When a couple is able to clear away any negativity that is between them through communication, counseling, or simple forgiveness, they find it much easier to get back to the feelings of appreciation and respect for each other. Without the unresolved negativity blocking their feelings of affection, couples are more inclined to want to be more intimate and sexual.

Couples who do not have an active or somewhat regular sex life need to get past their challenges to find a new appreciation, respect, and admiration for each other, which can lead to a renewed affection. This is possible through honest and straightforward communication about each others needs, concerns, feelings, and any resentments they may have.

Forgiveness and the healing of past wounds can occur when both people are motivated to try and are genuinely interested in creating a break-through. The sections on communication and conflict can help a couple accomplish this.

Once a couple begins to get back on track, they will often have new feelings of affection for each other. This can be the source of energy that stimulates a new interest and passion for sex between them. This is made possible by a shift in beliefs, perspectives, and attitudes, which sometimes occurs as a result of going through a bonding experience such as reading this book together.

Familiarity & Fantasies

While many couples must clear the path for this love to resurface, this is certainly not the only cause of a decline in a couple's sex life. Even partners who communicate and resolve problems effectively may find their passion and interest level diminish over the years.

Of all the reasons that couples lose much of their interest and appetite for sex with each other, none is more common, understandable, and impossible to avoid as "familiarity." As a couple becomes more and more comfortable with each other, chances improve that their feelings of "desire" will diminish. This is even more of a possibility if a couple's sex life becomes predictable and routine.

Even a rich, gooey brownie, which is typically savored & consumed with passion, if eaten every day, may eventually lose much of its appeal & intensity. The brownie doesn't change, but our appreciation for it can.

A couple's sex life *is* going to change over a long period of time. Many people eventually wonder, "Is it just my relationship that's losing its spark, or is it inevitable?" It is a very rare couple that manages to maintain that edge and intensity over a lifetime. The intensity may last longer in some relationships than in others. Yet the kind of desire that was present at the very beginning will change and take other forms.

I'm not saying passion will die and there's nothing you can do about it. On the contrary, the "desire" will simply change from when you first met. Love-making can continue to be enjoyable and satisfying, but the *feeling of being desired* that most people fantasize about typically changes over time. Your passion can evolve into affection and a deeper level of love and connection. A couple may still find sex to be a powerful expression of love and an intense physical and emotional experience. It's the "desire" that is normally associated with new relationships that changes with familiarity.

When two people become so comfortable with each other that their sex lives become relatively predictable, that initial "desire" can begin to diminish. At this stage, one or both partners may start to worry about their relationship. Most, after a period of time, come to accept this reduced drive and passion and settle for "maintenance sex." It is possible to keep an intensity and passion alive in your relationship by staying in love, which is the object of this book. Yet the "lust and desire" that occurs in a new relationship *will* change over time.

Because many people miss that rush and excitement that can occur between new couples in love, some begin having fantasies of desire that may include their partner, or even a friend, an acquaintance, or maybe even a complete stranger. Having sexual fantasies does not mean that you don't love your partner. Instead it simply means that you are feeling the need to be desired.

To understand and interpret fantasies, you only need to look for the *underlying content of what happens*. It's not very important where the story takes place, what you're wearing, or what season it is. By looking past the "storyline" to the basic meaning of most fantasies, you will usually see a common theme; one person is intensely desired by another.

Since truly committed couples in long-term, monogamous relationships don't act on fantasies that involve anyone other than their partner, there is a good possibility these fantasies may persist for a great part of their lives. Those who have pursued their fantasies usually say that their extra-marital trysts were not as great as they imagined them to be, and the feeling of being desired only lasted for a few moments. Many have told me they found the experience to be hollow and lacking of any depth of feeling compared to being with their partner who they knew well and genuinely loved.

Longing to be desired by others may occasionally diminish one's interest in their sex life with their partner. If this sounds like you, it is important that you get back to focusing on why you love your partner and how much you appreciate having him/her in your life. Familiarity can not be reversed, yet it is possible to reframe what it means and instead embrace the fact that you have a wonderful partner whom you know, love, and are comfortable with.

The appreciation and affection you feel for your partner is based upon all of the love you have shared for years together. It is much deeper and more meaningful than the surface attraction between two people who barely know each other. Remember when the two of you first met. Think back to all of the adventures, experiences, and memories that you have shared over the years. Look for the attributes of your partner that you've come to admire and respect. Notice the peace and comfort you feel when lying in each other's arms. Express this affection in your words, touch, and presence when you are together intimately.

By embracing familiarity and continually feeling
the appreciation you have for your partner you create
the basis for long-term passion in your relationship.

The "M" Word

Another less common but yet important reason for a depleted sex drive is masturbation. While not always the case, the sexual "tension" that builds within a person is often relieved by masturbation. If a person masturbates frequently, it can significantly diminish their drive to make love with their partner.

Since many adults still feel uncomfortable discussing the topic of masturbation, it's not uncommon for people to be "secretive" about masturbating. When a person is feeling the need to connect with their partner on a sexual level but their partner has little or no interest, it is often misinterpreted, and can lead to anxiety, worry, or even anger. One may take it personally, when their partner may simply be masturbating regularly, leaving them uninterested in having sex.

Masturbation is only a problem when a couple's sex life begins suffering because of the resulting lack of interest. If this is your situation, then your relationship would benefit if you masturbate less frequently. If you feel the urge, sometimes it helps to simply distract yourself by becoming involved in a project, watching a movie, or getting some physical exercise. That way, when you are then together with your partner you will still have much of the energy and interest in sex as you had earlier. Although you may want to masturbate, it is possible to be patient and wait to share this sexual energy with your partner. The most important point to remember is moderation, and to make certain that you don't divert all of your energy away from your partnership.

The Imbalance

Because we all look at the world and interpret situations differently, it is quite common for one person in a partnership to feel their sex life together has diminished and is lackluster while the other believes everything is "fine."

Since what we all want and need sexually is so individual, the only true means of assessing whether or not there is a problem is if you or your partner feels there is. If your partner is not satisfied or wants change, that's really what matters and needs to be discussed. Considering that you want the person you love to be happy, it would be valuable for you to acknowledge and respect their perspective, even if you don't see the situation in the same manner.

It's also quite common that one of the two partners in a relationship will have a larger appetite for sex than the other. If this is true in your partnership, as long as the difference isn't light years apart, you can manage just fine. However, if this imbalance is extreme and grows to the point of one partner becoming frustrated, bored, or resentful, then it becomes a problem for both individuals.

If a *major* imbalance of interest in sex continues for too long, the dissatisfied partner will probably grow restless, eventually losing interest in having sex with their partner. This isn't to say that if your partner wants to have sex constantly you must go along, even if you don't want to. But finding a way to compromise and achieving a balance is important.

If one person never or very rarely wants to have sex, as a couple they need to discuss why this situation exists. If the uninterested partner doesn't know why, I highly recommend seeing a counselor to look more closely at their thoughts and feelings regarding sex and intimacy.

People who are healthy and want to feel alive tend to like and enjoy sex and the connection that brings with another person. If they are in a committed relationship that is absent of this intimacy and intensity, chances are pretty good they will either come to resent their partner or someday begin to look around at the possibility of having a satisfying sex life again - with someone else.

Understanding there is often a minor imbalance in our sexual drives makes it bearable that the imbalance is present. But it doesn't mean that it should be entirely ignored or accepted. Instead the person who wants more sex might compromise and learn to be satisfied with less than what is *optimal*, but not necessarily less than they *need*. It would also be beneficial for their less enthusiastic partner to be willing to initiate sex occasionally, and to sometimes stretch to give their partner more sex and/or intimacy than they need themselves.

If one's lack of desire for sex is based upon the fact their partner is doing very little to capture their interest or there are unresolved problems as mentioned above, then, as a couple, this must be addressed.

One could build a reasonable case that sex is over-rated and too important to society or to their partner. Yet sex is and will remain a part of our lives that must be acknowledged as being important enough to eventually end a relationship if it is absent. Do what it takes to rekindle it, or to keep it an alive and a vital part of your relationship.

Relationships and marriages can and do end up being discarded just because of a lack of a mutual commitment to a compatible sex life. Even when both partners are committed, it is easy to get busy and go for periods of time without sharing much sex. Communication is essential to being successful in achieving balance and getting back on track. Sometimes people think they shouldn't have to talk about having sex, it should just happen spontaneously.

If my wife is feeling the need to connect with me, she simply needs to let me know how she's feeling. The way Kris approaches me encourages me to want to do something about it. If I think we need to have sex or some intimate time together, I must make my intentions and needs known as well. Sometimes when I speak up she is actually feeling the same way and is glad to hear it is important to me too.

The imbalance can shift back and forth between partners over their years together. There may be times when one craves more sex and intimacy and their partner is distracted or has temporarily lost interest. As partners and as a team, it is important for both to take the initiative to keep your sexual life strong and healthy when either of you senses a significant imbalance is occurring.

Taking Responsibility

Reviving or maintaining the intimacy and sexual connection between a couple is not always easy. Since some couples don't always know how to do so or believe it's even possible, they make the mistake of avoiding the challenge by just starting over with a different partner. They cast aside the relationship in which they had invested so much time and energy because of an absence of regular and satisfying sex for one that is new and full of desire.

Chances are their new relationship will grow to be familiar and predictable as well. It's an art keeping sex alive and interesting over a long period of time. If one can't figure out how to do so in their current relationship, the same problem will just re-surface in their next one.

When there is a significant imbalance or the overall sex life has diminished or disappeared, some people make no attempt to do anything about it or only put in a token effort towards change. When the results are not immediate, they conclude that their relationship is doomed to remain the same. Unless they have really made serious, consistent attempts at creating the changes in their relationship that they both need to feel satisfied, they're cheating themselves by walking away.

If your sex life is non-existent or boring at best, what have you done about it? What responsibility have you taken, what attempts have you made to create serious change - beyond surface efforts such as an occasional romantic gesture or trying to initiate sex a couple of times?

Without an extraordinary commitment to keep *sex and intimacy* part of your lives, you can unconsciously let this important aspect of your relationship disappear. Two people who possess solid communication skills and are both committed to creating and sustaining intimacy simply do not allow themselves to expend all of their energy on everything *but* intimate time together. Scheduling intimacy time and discussing how you can be better lovers is important.

After work, meals, and children, it's easy to be drained of energy and uninterested in sex. Sleep can be much more enticing. Occasionally, changing your daily habits in order to leave energy or make the time for each other can be a valuable practice. For example, suppose you're in the habit of eating a large dinner which usually leaves you feeling tired. Once in a while plan on making love on a particular evening, and make sure that night your dinner is very light. Even better, if at all possible, enjoy having sex *before* dinner.

Another example of an adjustment that can be made is to plan some intimate time during the day. If children are an issue, make arrangements to have them taken care of so this may be possible. Get away for some weekends, just the two of you.

Some couples also find themselves glued to the television until they are totally out of energy or until it's late and they must go right to sleep since they need to get up early for work. Why not occasionally turn the tube off an hour or two before you normally go to bed? The two of you can go to bed earlier than usual so you can be awake together. These simple examples are just a few minor daily adjustments that can help you keep your sexual relationship active and alive.

People typically don't want to accept responsibility for aspects of their life that are less than perfect. Some like to be "victims" who are powerless to create change in their lives and instead find it easier to blame their boring or sexless relationship on their partner. Since they believe their own perspective is accurate, they point fingers and make no progress. But the real responsibility lies within each of us.

Truly committed couples are comprised of two partners who will both make the effort to communicate through whatever obstacles may stand in the way of a satisfying and fulfilling sex life.

If you have needed major change in your intimate and sexual relationship and already have made what you thought was a heroic effort to make change occur but to no avail, try again after you've finished this book. For other couples, keep making the effort to let your partner know how you feel by sharing frequent and meaningful *intimacy.*

The heart of the matter is, the more focused you are on your partner and what you love about him/her, the more involved and interested in being sexual with them you will be. Having a sexless relationship doesn't just happen to people. We all make choices regarding how we spend our energy and express ourselves to our partners.

Chances are what you both really want out of sex is the feeling of being loved, desired, and wanted, expressed physically. You know why interest fades and what you can do about it. The real question is what will you actually do about keeping the passion and excitement alive in your relationship? Remember to take responsibility yourself. The more respect, love, and appreciation you express, the more you will feel and experience in return.

~

CHAPTER 19

The Temptation Tightrope
Dealing with the lure of sexual attraction

~

Life is full of surprises, making it impossible to know what's just around the corner. Even if you are in love and happily married, you can by chance meet someone that you find yourself attracted to. The frequency of such an occurrence will be different for everyone, as well as the intensity of the emotions and feelings that an unexpected encounter can bring. Although you may not do anything about the stir you feel, the pull of a mutual attraction is still a force that must be dealt with.

Some idealistic romantics would like to believe that a person who is truly in love will never find themselves drawn to another person. There are many wonderful, personable, and beautiful people in the world. Over the course of a lifetime, the odds are pretty good that you will eventually meet at least a few people that you are intrigued by, regardless of whether you're happy in your relationship or not.

A couple's love and the solidity of their relationship can play a major role in keeping them true to their partnership. However, if a couple is struggling and has been for a while, it's a dangerous reality that one or both partners may rationalize having an affair. A tempted person may think they have a good rationale for straying, yet the bottom line is it would be better if he/she resisted the easy fix and instead tried to resolve their problems and renew their love for their partner.

Affairs

Unfortunately, affairs do occur in a great many relationships today, and normally are the result, not the cause, of the breakdown of the relationship. Some begin because one person may be missing companionship, intellectual stimulation, or an emotional connection with their mate. Others occur because of the lack of a fulfilling and satisfying sexual relationship between the two partners. Because it's not always easy for couples to improve or revive their sex life, often they begin looking outside of their relationship to fill the void.

Many relatively solid marriages have been abandoned, families torn apart, and careers have been destroyed by the lure of sexual attraction to a person outside of the partnership. An unknown but certainly significant percentage of marriages do not survive affairs.

Some people believe they just need to "get this urge out of their system." But an affair usually begins to weaken one's involvement and connection to their partner. A person who finds themself rationalizing his/her behavior is more apt to rationalize having extra-marital sex again in the future. The foundation continues to weaken as they begin lying to their partner. Self-respect decreases and sense of guilt increases, further distancing them emotionally from their partner.

For couples who want to do their best to stay in love and together, obviously it's important to take each other's wants and needs seriously. A willingness to be open to sharing your feelings and thoughts as well as listening to your partner is essential, especially regarding the sensitive area of sex.

Take measures to strengthen your connection and make the effort to keep your love and passion alive throughout your years together. Your desire to stray will be minimal to non-existent because you will have virtually all of your needs met. You may still find yourself attracted to another person occasionally, but you'll be very clear that the sexual energy is only a small piece of the whole pie. Because your partnership will be so satisfying in every department, you would be crazy to risk losing the complete package for a surface attraction.

The Primal Urge

Recently my wife and I were invited to be on a talk show with another author whose book suggested that men were genetically compelled to seek out multiple partners in order to insure the propagation of the human species. His research implied that men were almost powerless because of this "primal urge" and that it is instinctive for them to want to have sex with multiple partners. This opinion provides a weak but easy excuse for men who want to use it to justify their actions since they were "simply following their instincts."

While it may true that a majority of men would enjoy having multiple sexual partners, and this may possibly be related to our ancestry, men do have the power to not act upon their urges. Even if there is some merit to this propagation theory historically, I believe that men and women in the 20th century are able to override most of their sexual instincts by using their intellects.

We are not held hostage to this primal urge. People can choose to commit to a monogamous relationship and follow through because of their values, sense of integrity, and love for their partner. If anything, some people do not stay loyal simply because they are not totally committed emotionally to doing so. They may say the words and make some of the gestures, but emotionally they remain partially committed.

Sagging Self-Image

Psychology is basically the study of how our thinking effects our actions. Understanding the psychology behind affairs is important because a person's thinking can create the rationalizations which makes it possible to take actions that may be regretted later. This is especially true when someone is in a committed relationship but is looking outside the relationship to have their self-image boosted and sexual interests satisfied.

It's not uncommon for people who are beginning to age to experience a sagging self-image. Since we can't help but notice the physical signs of aging, many people become increasingly concerned about their attractiveness and seek confirmation that they still have something to offer, something of interest to others. This partially explains the frequent incidence of older men and women having sexual affairs with younger people. They often think, "If this young man or woman, who could have plenty of young, attractive partners wants me, I must still be desirable."

Yet even some young people who are not experiencing any "aging trauma" may need constant affirmation that they are attractive and desirable. While remembering that not all people will struggle with this, it's important to acknowledge the need to be seen as attractive. Obviously not everyone ends up having affairs as they age. What's essential is what a person ultimately does about their need to be desired.

If you are feeling insecure about your attractiveness, know that finding another person besides your partner who finds you desirable is not the cure. Eventually, you will probably feel the same concern because this one new person with whom you would become involved is only that, one person. A sagging self-image can not be permanently remedied by finding a new lover.

Flirting

We all know it can be fun and interesting to meet someone with whom we share a mutual attraction. Some people can find enough satisfaction in a little occasional flirting, and having an affair is never really considered an option. A little occasional playful flirting can be quite harmless. This exchange between two people can provide some reinforcement that others find them attractive. Most of this is simply an innocent part of being alive. Wouldn't you admit that you like the feeling?

Yet flirting can be a problem when someone insults their partner by flirting in front of them. It can also be a problem when a person in a committed relationship is addicted to flirting, sacrificing an inordinate amount of time, energy, money, or all of the above on its pursuit.

Flirting can also be dangerous because sometimes the intensity of the attraction can impair the ability of those involved to keep their situation in perspective. Sometimes a person can get so caught up in flirting that they bypass their reasoning and consciousness of their surroundings. Values may be put away in a box and sealed tight, only to be taken out afterwards. Even significant priorities such as marriages can be temporarily forgotten or ignored while in this state.

It is helpful for a person to learn how to be satisfied with a simple and occasional flirt. Keep it short and don't get carried away. After all, it is an interesting part of being alive. Chances are you're going to flirt at least a little, so give up the idea that you or anyone can just wish that impulse away. But most importantly, make the acknowledgment that someone else is interested in you be enough and satisfying in itself. You may get the affirmation that others see you as attractive through some occasional flirting, yet remain clear that the love between you and your partner is much more important and worth preserving.

Some are good at listening to the wisdom they have accumulated, while others are masters at shutting it off. We may all have many of the same primal tendencies - but some people *allow* themselves to lose control. We're not helpless in this situation. Others have demonstrated commitment and will power to find the inner strength to pull out of a situation that starts deepening, that starts looking like there could be consequences that could seriously undermine their best interests in their careers, family, and marriage.

Where this inner strength comes will vary for everyone. Some find the strength in their sense of integrity, as this is important enough to them to shape their decisions and thinking. Your friends, values, morals, or your spirituality can help you avoid this trap and support you in staying on track. Your love and respect for your partner can keep you focused on the relationship you are committed to.

The Bottom Line

Aside from all of the reasons that lead to people having affairs, the reality is: the pleasure may be intense, but it doesn't last. For example, ten minutes after eating a fresh chocolate chip cookie you can no longer feel the pleasure that you had just experienced. All you have left is the calories and fat. The thrill of an extra-marital sexual encounter is also usually short-lived and reality comes crashing down soon afterwards. What is left is the guilt, baggage, and a faded memory.

Affairs are by far one of the most difficult challenges for couples to overcome emotionally. An affair destroys the trust and weakens the entire foundation of the bridge that connects a couple intimately. Some people don't clearly see the emptiness of their actions until it's too late.

They find their thirst was not quenched by the follow-through on their desires. Too many recognize afterwards how much they really had, and how lucky they really were.

If you're not happy with your sex life, experiencing a turn-around isn't just a matter of learning new "techniques." More "routine" sex is not what would satisfy you. Chances are it's the underlying passion, love, and intensity that you miss. A couple who is bored or unhappy with their sex life needs to look at the causes of their problem instead of trying to remedy the situation by being more "creative" sexually or simply increasing the frequency of having intercourse.

Good Sex Is In The Head

There's little question as to the most important part of your anatomy when it comes to sexual satisfaction - the head on your shoulders. All of your anatomy may be related to your *experience*, but each part by itself has little to do with your overall feeling of sexual arousal. The brain is always interpreting what is happening sexually between a couple. Your brain searches for signs of passion. When you detect a lack of passion from your partner, no matter how he/she touches you or what is said, it can be almost impossible to find the experience "exciting."

The return of "passion" is always dependent on trust and shifts in attitude and emotional involvement.

Some couples may love each other very much but have unconsciously allowed themselves to get in a rut sexually. Without intending to become lazy and predictable, they unknowingly send signals of a lukewarm interest in sex with each other. These couples usually don't work too hard to rejuvenate their sex life together. For couples such as this, it is extremely helpful to save more energy for sex, to be more present with why and how much they love their partner, and to be more committed to expressing affection and conveying desire.

When one partner is feeling the lack of desire and passion, this is very important and steps should be taken to remedy the situation. The first step is communicating in a straightforward yet diplomatic manner, remembering to avoid using any blame or other negative messages.

Communicate what is desired, such as more expressiveness and involvement, instead of illustrating how the partner is failing miserably as a lover. Avoid using words such as uninteresting and apathetic. Find a way to gracefully point out unconscious messages from your partner. Most importantly, *consider what you are conveying to your partner in regards to how you feel about them.*

Is making love with you a distant and unemotional experience because you're only partially there? Are you in the habit of doing many of the same things, at the same times, in the same ways, as if following a blueprint, so that you can successfully accomplish orgasm? Are you a passive partner who let's things be done to them, or simply takes requests or commands and performs for their partner? Do you consciously communicate, through your touch, a sincere affection and love for your partner? Do you save energy and show enthusiasm for sex, or does your partner have to survive on the half-awake variety? Does the way you hold, kiss, hug, and make love with your partner express a strong affection and attraction?

Couples have told me, "We have sex on a regular basis, so our sex life must be O.K." Yet while they are having sex they sometimes send unintentional messages that don't convey passion or affection, which is why they often don't feel satisfied afterwards. We all want to be desired, loved, and to experience passion and intimacy. If both partner's feel desired, they will probably share a powerful experience.

If one believes they are simply going "through the routine," they may lose interest or feel unfulfilled afterwards. The entire experience hinges on what they each "decide" is happening, which is why your brain is the most important part of your sexual anatomy. For couples in long-term relationships, the meaning must be there for the sex to be consistently satisfying and fulfilling.

Remember when you made love with your partner the first or second time? What was that experience like? What kind of lover were you then, versus what you were like the last time you made love? Chances are you put a lot more energy and life into those first times being intimate together. If you want to, it is possible to reclaim that enthusiasm, intensity, and sensuality. Although you'll never be able to fully recreate that first experience, with a little effort you can enjoy a *different* but even more deeply satisfying sexual intimacy with each other.

Even if you are both relatively happy with your sex life, why not see if you can't be even more present, more expressive, and more alive than you already are. Read the next chapter, in which you'll find a few additional and simple ways to improve your sexual connection with your partner. Putting more life and passion into your sex life changes your attitude and increases the amount of energy that you bring to being intimate and making love. Don't wait for your partner to change things for you. Take the initiative and strive to be a loving partner with whom you have already invested so much.

~

Chapter 20

Tune-Up Tips

Improving Your Sexual Connection

~

Establishing a healthy sexual and intimate connection with your partner is a multi-faceted endeavor. In this chapter you will first consider some of the sexual roles that lead to dissatisfaction in which people occasionally fall into. If you see yourself or your partner in one of these roles, it would be valuable to try breaking out of it. Doing so would require talking about your sexual relationship, the second focus of this chapter, followed by some favorite helpful hints for tuning -up your sexual interaction.

Couples who have a satisfying sex life together typically have a healthy and positive attitude regarding sex. A fulfilling sex life is often the result of a process of growth over many years in which couples mature individually as well as together. Being a compatible sexual companions and lovers is not necessarily instinctive, but more often the result of learning about ourselves and the opposite gender. Since we are each so different, sometimes it can take a while for couples to develop a clear understanding of what their particular partner likes and dislikes. This is much easier for couples who can comfortably talk about sex.

Yet not every couple finds it easy to communicate freely about their sex life. When this is the case, certain patterns can become established that may create a few problems. In order to get past these obstacles to a mutually satisfying sex life, occasionally a person may need to unlearn old "lessons" and shed old habits.

The following section briefly describes six common "roles" that people may assume. If any of these resemble you it would be extremely beneficial to make the effort to break your pattern.

1] Batteries Need Replacing

Passion is important in every aspect of a couples life together. Yet it seems to have a special significance in their sexual relationship. A passive and apathetic lover can be very frustrating to be with. For the person who is trying to make love with their somewhat lifeless partner, the sexual experience can easily escalate from disappointing to annoying. They usually end up feeling they are imposing themselves on their partner, and are doing something to him/her against their will instead of sharing a loving exchange.

There can be many reasons why one's partner is timid or seems uninterested in the bedroom. It's quite common for people, especially women, to have been raped, molested, or abused in some manner in their past. They may also emotionally shut down when it comes to sex because of insecurities regarding their attractiveness or ability. Out of fear they freeze up and distance themselves from their partner. It is important that a couple with this problem takes their intimate life seriously enough to get support from a qualified counselor. Many of the other "roles" people may fall into are less complicated and can often be avoided by a conscious choice and effort to do so.

2] And Now Performing....

These people think sex is like a stage, and they must perform for and impress their partners. They enjoy bragging about how long they can go or how many orgasms they had or helped their partner have. Unlike those who need a little more energy, they have an abundance.

The problem is this "performance" is a way to avoid being intimate and emotionally involved with their partner. It's safer and more comfortable for this person to hide behind their performance than it is if they were to be more real and genuinely loving and affectionate. Breaking this habit can be challenging but is certainly possible. Couples will find it especially beneficial to periodically spend some intimate time in bed together without the sex and orgasms.

3.] The Perfectionist

Everything has to be just right for these compulsive lovers. The music, the lighting, the entire setting has to be perfect. Often the way they are touched has to be done according to an imaginary script, and if anything is out of place or not done in the proper sequence or intensity, they're sure to be unable to "get in the mood."
The perfectionist is often very controlling in other areas of life. Establishing rigid patterns has killed the spontaneity and sexual enjoyment between many couples. It is important the perfectionist learns to let go of their expectations and rigid beliefs about the way "things need to be" and become more comfortable with imperfections, variety, and surprise.

4.] Following Directions

A "cousin" to the perfectionist is the lover who must have everything performed in a certain manner. They constantly issue commands or give directions. "Touch me here, a little harder, over to the right, not like that, like this ...." While it's healthy to occasionally guide and inform your partner to help them learn what you enjoy, if this becomes a continual pattern it will turn sex into a "procedure."

As with the perfectionist, this type of a lover will make it very hard for his/her partner to become emotionally involved in making love because of always being worried about "doing it right" and following directions. Instead of sex being an exchange of intimacy, it will eventually feel more like you're completing a project or task. It's important for couples who have this challenge to be quieter and more spontaneous, learning how to just let their intimacy and love making "flow."

5] Anything For You

"How does this feel? Do you like that? How does it feel now?" These statements can be heard repeatedly in the bedroom of the partner that will do anything for you. Their focus is solely upon their partner's pleasure, not on what feels good to them or on the bigger picture, making love and exchanging intimacy. They are not "connected" to their partner emotionally, but instead are focused on the technical aspect of the sex.

Balance is just as important in a couple's sexual relationship as elsewhere in life. Making love is more exciting and enjoyable when two people are able to see to it that they both experience pleasure and satisfaction regularly. It can be just as fun for both people to give as well as to receive. This "selflessness" is honorable in small doses but on a regular basis robs both people of the full range of enjoyment and intimacy that is possible.

6) All For Me, Nothing for You

This refers to partners who don't seem to be interested in anyone's pleasure and satisfaction other than their own. The opposite of the previous example, these lovers concentrate *only* on what they want, what feels good to them, and achieving orgasms when they want to.

It is extremely satisfying to be "together" when making love. While not everyone will have "mutual orgasms simultaneously," when one person ignores his/her partner's state of arousal and is only interested in their own orgasms, sex becomes impersonal and unappealing. It can be very helpful for this person to slow down when orgasm is approaching to "let their partner catch up" and also concentrate on his/her partner's pleasure more often. After all, an island can be a lonely place if it's inhabited by only one person.

~

If any of the above "roles" sounds like you or your partner, it's important to break through this pattern and establish a sexual relationship that is more healthy and balanced. This can be accomplished through a mutual willingness to be open and share what you each feel, and by truly listening to each other without becoming angry or defensive. If you try to achieve a breakthrough on your own and still find it difficult after both of you have read this book, look for a good counselor in your area who can help.

Talking About Sex

It's my experience that the most challenging subject overall for people to talk about with their partners is sex. In the right situation, with the right friend, many men and women have no problem being open with their thoughts, feelings, and experiences regarding sex. But when it comes to talking about sex with their partner, everything changes.

Thus, it doesn't take a rocket scientist to conclude that the only reason we can't talk about sex with our partner is the inner dialogue we have which tells us that doing so could be dangerous. This belief may be based upon previous unsuccessful attempts at discussing sex. Talking about sex can be similar to walking through a mine field, not knowing where it's safe to go and where it's not. For some this could mean receiving disapproval and starting a conflict with their partner. To others they are afraid of hurting their partner's feelings. Many would rather live in disappointment and be a "victim" who is not loved enough, or in the way that they want to be, than risk talking it through.

Many of the suggestions presented in the chapters on communication can be applied when talking about your sexual relationship with your partner. As in speaking a new language, the discomfort seems to dissipate over time when you get more accustomed to trying. What makes this easier is the "safety" factor.

Remember, safety is knowing that your partner is going to listen without becoming unreasonably upset at what they hear, and knowing he/she will reciprocate and respond with his/her own thoughts or feelings. Safety is a generalized assessment of how you feel your partner can and probably will react to your attempt to communicate. Safety is never assured, nor can it be guaranteed.

Believing your partner will probably make talking about an emotionally sensitive and vulnerable issue safe helps give you the strength to try walking through the mine field. Men *and* women need to work at making it very safe for their partner to say *anything* if they are interested in the truth, in growth, and being the lover that their partner deserves and wants in their life.

At times we get messages from our partner that simply hurt. Egos may get bruised, or perceptions of reality called into question. Some of your partner's comments may hit you where you are the most sensitive, like a dentist poking around in your mouth and finding a cavity or exposed nerve. Here you need an extra dose of a commitment to making it safe.

Resist your fight or flight reflex which would evaporate the safety immediately. In these moments, it is also critical that you silence your inner lawyer who may want to jump to your defense. Try to resist the compelling urge to "counter" with an attack or point out flaws in your partner's perceptions. This is done by remembering that your partner is explaining how he/she would feel more loved. Simply be a concerned and attentive listener.

When sharing personal views, thoughts, or feelings with your partner, keep in mind that demanding or expecting safety does not always make it happen. Review the chapters on communication, and consider using the tools mentioned. You can reduce the possibility of hurting his/her feelings or creating a defensive stance from your partner. Honesty can be achieved without having to be brutal, demeaning, or inconsiderate. This is a skill that needs to be developed for most people however, and if your partner steps on your toes, chances are he/she didn't mean to. The spirit of forgiveness truly helps create and maintain this safety.

With a genuine opening for listening between the two of you, it will be much easier to mutually create the intimate life you both desire. It will take both of you to not only listen well, but to also put something at stake by taking a risk and expressing your own thoughts, feelings, and needs as well. The more you do so, the easier it becomes, until you reach the point where someday you laugh about how hard it used to be!

A final suggestion: Reserve your discussions about your sex life for times when you're not in bed. If you have any sensitive issues which need to be talked about, bring them up at a neutral time when you're both in a good mood & not trying to resolve any problems or other issues.

Techniques That Work

On a day to day basis, there are many very simple and timeless things a couple can do to for mini-tune-ups or pleasure enhancements in the privacy of their own home, which cost nothing, and are also quite valuable. Here are my favorite five:

1.] What I Love About You

One of the best gifts anyone can give their partner is a list of things they love about them. Focus on the attributes of your partner that you really appreciate and respect them for. What makes him/her better than the others of their gender, in your opinion? What special gifts do they have? What things do they do that makes it easy to love them? Giving such a list to your partner is always treasured, and helps you consciously focus on the gift they are to your life as well.

This acknowledgment is one of the best forms of non-physical foreplay. While you are laying in bed holding each other closely, think of one or two of the things that would be on your list, and mention them to your partner. A sure way to bring you closer to each other is to mention what you love about each other.

Another great gesture is to bring up some of the most enjoyable times you've shared together as a couple. Visualize a day you spent together that was one of your favorites, and picture being there again with your partner. Whether it was a celebration, a day on vacation, or just a downright steamy lovemaking session, put yourself back in that place, and then let them in on what you've been thinking about.

2.] Make A Pact

A great way to get back on track if you're experiencing a dip in sexual activity is to agree on a "pact" for making love with your partner. What works best is when you both decide on a specific number of days, say five in a row, that you *will* make love together. This must be a "no matter what" deal. The two of you make adjustments in your schedules or get creative if necessary in order to do what it will take to achieve successful completion of the arrangement.

If you set out a specified number of days and both stick to it, you'll be amazed at how fun it can be and how easy it really is to do. The time of day may need to vary, maybe even the location. Chances are you will have to plan when and where your next day's interlude will take place in order to see success. Try it just for fun if for no other reason. I suggest that busy couples who have challenging lifestyles and schedules do this a couple times a year just for a good solid dose of lovin'!

3.] Yellow Light

Everyone knows that a flashing yellow light means slow down and proceed with caution. This message is perfect for the couple who is already in the process of making love and would like to extend the pleasurable experience. When one person is rapidly approaching the point of orgasm, they simply need to say, "Yellow," which cues their partner to slow down or maybe even to stop moving altogether.

This allows the person who is at the "yellow" stage to relax and calm down slightly, enabling them to resume making love without rushing into orgasm. Since it is rare that couples will have perfect timing and always have orgasms together, this technique sometimes allows the other partner to "catch up." After going through a yellow or two, both people may find they are both ready to have an orgasm and can then enjoy proceeding towards experiencing one together.

The key is to not wait too long before saying, "Yellow," since there is a point of no return. Also, quite often people are afraid they'll "lose" the orgasm by stopping. If your partner doesn't mind using this technique, and you try it a few times together, I think you'll discover that you never lose the orgasm. Once you are at that stage, it doesn't take too much to get right back to the same point you left off at.

Since many couples don't have sex with a lot of frequency, when they *are* making love, why not extend it and make last? Achieving orgasms are not the sole purpose of sex, but certainly a nice part of it. Why rush through it? When one person says, "Yellow," they are saying, "Don't move, I want this moment with you to last longer." It's then time to breathe, hold on to each other, laugh, or run your fingers through your partner's hair. When your partner says it's safe to proceed, do so slowly and with caution. Most importantly, have fun!

4.] The Twenty Second Kiss

The twenty second kiss is a long, slow, deliberate kiss. This is by no means a new idea, but one that is worthwhile nonetheless. Many couples eventually move from a regular diet of passionate kissing to routine lip pecks, reserving their passionate kissing for special occasions.

The length of this kiss makes it special. You don't have to reserve the twenty second kiss for the bedroom. It can be perfect before your partner is leaving to go somewhere, upon their arrival at home, or at anytime other time. Just ask for it by name, "Honey, I want a 20 second kiss, please." How can one's partner say no? I do recommend however, that you never ask for a twenty second kiss after eating Gorgonzola cheese or Oreo cookies.

"Kissing is a means of getting two people so close together that they can't see anything wrong with each other."
Rene Yasenek

5.] The Sixty Second Hug

The sixty second hug is a wonderful way to say good-bye or to reconnect with each other after being separated during your days, and is a sweet way to express a non-sexual intimacy with each other. Don't be precise and exact about the time. Instead the basic idea is that you commit to at least a minute of a full body hug. When you do, something sort of magical happens after about 35 seconds. You relax in each others arms and begin to really feel each other breathing, feel the softness of their skin, and sort of melt into each other. Again, just ask for a sixty second hug anytime you want to feel closer to your partner. It's easy, convenient, and affordable.

~

Couples who have been together for a long time and still love each other are a wonderful treat to run across. One of the key ingredients that they have, which is usually easy to spot, is an affection and appreciation for each other. Although that may sound simplistic, maintaining it is not necessarily easy.

People who spend a lot of time together usually find it easier to focus on their differences and get frustrated by each other's quirks and behaviors. But the couples who see beyond all of that and concentrate on what they do have together are the happy couples whom you may want to model your relationship after.

As the hours together turn into weeks, then months, and then years, you may stray a little off course even though you have the best intentions. Even couples who truly appreciate and respect each other can sometimes take each other for granted. It is in these times that it is helpful to do something different to re-awaken your conscious loving ability. That might be reading a book, doing a seminar, going on a vacation, or maybe even spending some time apart so that you will miss each other.

Whatever the solution may be for you, when one person starts feeling ambivalent about the relationship or one of you feels taken for granted, speak up and make a request for a little "attitude adjustment." Your intimacy & sexual relationship together is an important bridge to feel connected to the most important person in your life!

How Can Your Sex & Intimacy Improve ?

As we've mentioned throughout the chapters on sex and intimacy, communication is the key to keeping your sex life alive and healthy. Now that we've covered a range of potential issues that may be relevant to your partnership, I encourage you to both take the next step and have an in-depth and personal discussion about this part of your life together. In order to make this easier and more focused, complete the questionnaire that follows. It would be a good idea to do this every now and then just to make sure that everything is on the table and you both are aware of each other's perceptions and feelings. Information such as this gives you a more clear idea of a direction to take in keeping your sexual and intimate life a fulfilling source of satisfaction and pleasure.

Write down on a separate sheet of paper the number of the following questions and the corresponding answers as you see them. Be honest and frank. These questions are designed to have you take a look at, from different angles, where you currently stand and where you can grow together. If one of your answers seems to already have been written in a previous answer, move on to the next question.

1) Do you have any general sexual complaints about your partner or your sex life?

2) Do you regularly have any feelings of insecurities regarding yourself, including your body or lovemaking that may effect your ability to be sexual or intimate?

3) Is there anything you are afraid to talk about, to say, or ask for from your partner?

4) Does your partner think you enjoy a particular sexual activity that you don't? If so, what?

5) What you would like more or less of?

6) What do you like the most about your sexual life together, and the least?

7) I feel the closest to you when.......

8) I feel distant from you when.....

9) What could *you* do yourself to improve your sex life that would help you be more satisfied?

Find a time to each share your answers with each other in regards to these questions. Be honest and open, yet be careful to be considerate and diplomatic at the same time. This area is sensitive for most people, and it's worthwhile to share your thoughts and feelings in a non-critical manner.

~

~

*"To be satisfied, each of us must know what he or she wants.
We can get our clothes or our meat off the rack, but sex should be
custom-tailored to order."*
Katherine Perutz

~

CHAPTER 21

The Good, Bad, & The Ugly

Living and loving during normal day to day life and challenging times

~

Special Occasions

The last two chapters are a collection of short sections relevant to partnership and everyday life, some of which are directed specifically to men or women.

The saying goes, "A little sensitivity goes a long way." Men don't need to become "Joe Sensitive" and begin to wear tights or act like they're part of a Harlequin romance novel. Yet there are times where a certain degree of sensitivity to what the woman in their life wants can be well worth the effort that a man may put forth.

While birthdays, anniversaries, and other special events may not be a big deal to some men, often they are to a woman. When this is the case, men would do well to be sensitive to the importance and significance that their partner places on the occasion. By making the effort to honor her feelings and interests, a man does not compromise his masculinity but instead shows a depth to his personality and presence.

Recently I was having dinner in a nice, quiet restaurant. A couple was sitting at the table next to me. The man was taking his wife out for her birthday. After dinner, she wanted a specific dessert which was not on the menu, and was hoping he would take her to a place that she knew offered it. Unfortunately her partner was tired and unenthusiastic. I heard her say, "Come on, the night is still young." I thought to myself, "Go for it! It's her birthday! Be the hero, take care of her, make her proud of you. She'll love the fact that you want her night to perfect!"

Many women have told me they don't want an overly sensitive man, yet would like their partner to not just be a "typical guy." They'd like it if he was occasionally romantic, expressive, and interesting. Consider how many men are predictable come Valentine's Day. They may give flowers or chocolates, a card, and maybe take their partner out to dinner.

A man doesn't need to be Shakespeare to write a personal note inside the card that expresses his appreciation and respect for the woman in his life. He can go the extra yard by having a nice bottle of wine and flowers at the table prior to their arrival at the restaurant. Or he could get a baby-sitter for the children and cook her a meal himself. Regardless of what he does, by going a little beyond the call of duty a man can express that his partner means a lot to him and he wanted to show it.

Since women are often more emotional than their partner, they tend to naturally get more interested, more involved, and more excited about milepost events. When men are blind to this reality or simply ignore this aspect of their partner, they make significant withdrawals from the "emotional bank account." While this may be unintentional, it isn't unavoidable.

Many men invalidate their woman's feelings by telling her she makes too big of a deal out of birthdays, anniversaries, etc., thus justifying his lack of effort and consideration.

While it may just seem like another day to some men, it may not be to his partner. By accusing her of over-reacting, some men make their partner wrong for being so excited about a special occasion. When men do this they may be able to appear right, and maybe get off the hook for not doing anything special or considerate. But it is clearly not a "win." It's really more of a loss in the long run, because they lost a chance to make a major deposit.Although all women are not romantics at heart, many are, and many appreciate it when a man honors that part of them.

When it is a woman's birthday, she appreciates it when the man in her life does more than just the minimum to get by and save face. By showing some effort around special occasions it will pay a man back ten fold in the long run because of the goodwill and appreciation she will have for him.

Sometimes the connection between a couple slowly leaks out as does the helium in a balloon over a few days. Couples may be left wondering, "Where did it go? What happened to us?" What they usually can't put their finger on is the source of their loss of passion and enthusiasm. Yet hundreds of times little withdrawals were made, little wounds were inflicted, and their lack of effort and focus over time allowed the feelings of being loved and appreciated to diminish.

Relationships don't end just because one person is not as excited and involved in a special event as their partner. But how we go through these special occasions does make an impact, positive or negative, that can build or deteriorate the connection between two people. If it's important to your partner, put in the extra effort. You may even learn how to make it fun for yourself in the process.

It's easy to create an average or typical relationship in which one or both partners put in minimal efforts and simply get by. But to have a "passionate partnership," both partners can't be lazy but instead must be more involved, put in more energy, and consistently generate surprise and interest by being unpredictable.

If you were just beginning to date you would probably show more effort than you currently do. If you already do a good job in this area, congratulations! Many of the secrets of keeping your love alive are in the little things. Why not make your next special occasion together memorable and have fun with it? Besides, it makes you more interesting and more lovable. After all, isn't life meant to be enjoyed? Get creative and make the time to express that you still care and that your partner is still your priority in life!

(As a side-note, Kris and I have an on-going agreement that when it's your birthday, you get to be "right" all day, no matter what! You might want to try it, it can provide a lot of laughs!)

Don't Forget About Dad

Many men could become more involved with their children so they wouldn't feel so much like an outsider. Men do have a responsibility for taking initiative and being an active participant in the parenting of their kids. It's not the women's job to make certain he is always happy. However, this section is written for the couple in which this isn't the issue. Instead it is focused on the woman who becomes so immersed in her children and being a mother that she accidentally begins to overlook and sometimes forgets about her connection and relationship with her partner.

Recently a woman came to see me and asked "My husband seems to be less patient and gets frustrated with me more now that we have a child. I thought it would be the opposite. Is this common?"

Consider the family with a very young "only child" who is used to getting all of the love and attention. What happens when they bring home a new baby? Quite often their child initially resents this new addition, since they get less of their parent's energy and attention.

A man can react much in the same manner once you have children. Intellectually he may know better, but emotionally he might feel like he is no longer the love of your life and feels replaced. Others feel used, as if their role was only to provide his partner with a child, and that it wasn't him that she really wanted.

This can happen when a woman continually shows the baby is the most important thing in her life, even more so than her relationship. If she is willing to sacrifice everything for the sake of their child, her man slips to a position of lesser value and importance. Emotionally the little boy inside him may resent this, which shows through in his impatience and frustrations.

Many women become so focused on their children that the man starts feeling lonely and not needed. Some men get so little attention and energy from their wives after children come on the scene that they begin to long for a relationship with a woman who finds *him* interesting and wants to be with him. Women need to be careful to not let this major imbalance occur or persist. *Continue to keep your relationship a priority,* and to express how much you value, appreciate, and love your partner.

Make efforts to include your man as much as possible, and not just in sharing the workload. Set aside time for just him alone to be the focus of your love and energy. After all, do you respect a person who works 80 hours a week to make their business a success and in the process destroys their health, marriage, and friendships? Don't put so much into your child that the relationship that created this miracle falls apart as a result.

Remember how your lives looked prior to entering the parenthood stage, and look for ways to keep some of that spontaneity, variety of conversation, and romance and intimacy alive.

In Sickness & In Health

It's easy to feel love for your partner when they are healthy and full of energy. Yet life may occasionally present you with times of sickness, which can be challenging even for those who deeply care and have all of the right intentions. How you get through those times is important to the overall "health" of your partnership.

Not every man or woman wants to be nurtured when they are sick. Some people prefer to be alone and get through it on their own. However, if your partner is not this way, be careful to be conscious of their needs and to be there for them when they are not feeling well. Suffocating your partner in times of need is not necessary, but letting them know how much you care and want to help will serve you both. While this may seem obvious, you'd be surprised at how many couples have problems in this area.

Some men, many of whom like to present an image of this independence and strength, are reduced to a meek helplessness when the flu bug really gets them. Many men have been raised with a caring mother figure in their childhood, and are more than comfortable having "Mother" take care of them. They may whine about their symptoms, and some expect to be waited on hand-and-foot. Yet many of these same men often forget about all of the nurturing they required when the woman in their life gets sick.

Debbie and Scott went through a frustrating period together before they came to see me. When Scott was sick, he had her make soup for him. She was getting cold medicine and cough drops. She was rubbing his sore muscles, and fetching him this and that. Upon his recovery, Debbie came down with what Scott had just gotten rid of.

Amazingly enough, his memory of his own recent high-maintenance period seemed to vanish. He was out playing golf, working late, and living life as usual. If anything, her symptoms seemed to annoy him and get on his nerves. Debbie was basically on her own. Scott figured she could take care of herself. Getting things for her, doing little things to be sweet, or even calling to check in with her seemed beyond his comprehension - and she was rightfully upset about it.

Granted, nurturing may come easily and naturally for most women. But a man who wants to go the extra mile and be a better husband and partner than most will rise to the occasion and make extra efforts to show their love for his partner when she becomes ill.

This can be especially important because in times such as these, a woman can easily feel abandoned, left to wonder how much her partner really loves her. She may fear that her unpleasant symptoms have driven her man away and created a distance between them.

Some may even worry about what might happen as she gets older and less attractive because of age, weight or illness - will he leave her? People who ignore or abandon their partners when they are having problems, emotionally or physically, weaken their partner's confidence in the relationship and faith in what the future holds for them as a couple.

To be fair, there are also many women who have not been raised to be *nurtured*, but rather to nurture. When this is the case, the woman requires little pampering, and sometimes simply doesn't like to be nurtured. Some women are not used to it and don't like it. This is particularly evident in the woman who, even when sick, is still taking care of everyone else, unable to bring herself to the "I need help" state.

One interesting positive side-effect of an unfortunate sickness is how the need for one's partner to help can actually bring a couple closer. One partner's empathy and consideration can sometimes move couples towards more of a connection. When one person becomes sick and needs help and one partner is forced to focus some loving energy on the other, this alone can snap them out of life on auto pilot.

Of course, if one's partner is *always* sick, the possibility for "bonding" becomes greatly reduced, and instead chances improve for a distance to occur between a couple. It can get old quickly when your partner is, for long periods of time or on a recurring basis, a miserable, sickly person. Some people, believe it or not, get sick intentionally to get attention, sympathy, or to feel some form of love.

Getting through the days when one partner is sick can be quite challenging. Especially when your partner's symptoms are somewhat revolting or unattractive. One hardly feels like being close to a person when they are constantly coughing, blowing their nose, or a variety of other less than appealing symptoms that my editor suggested I leave out. One of the best strategies is to try to find humor and make light of the situations. Too many people literally become angry when their partner is "being so disgusting."

Keep in mind that very rarely does your partner upset you on purpose by *not* treating you the way you might want them to. You may need to communicate about what you want, need, and expect from each other. When your partner is not showing you respect and they aren't being very thoughtful, try expressing this in a way that doesn't make them resentful or defensive.

Many women find true joy in giving, helping, and nurturing, and go on doing so without considering the cost.

Men, on the other hand, must often consciously choose to be there in such a manner for their partners.

Don't fall into the trap of thinking that a man's lack of nurturing is a definitive symbol of his lack of love because he's simply following his auto-pilot. Having your partner rise to the occasion and help you out may take some work initially, but gives them an opportunity to win major points with you and to have a chance to be proud of themselves.

Loving people who are sick isn't always easy, but in the long-term it's worth going out of your way to honor their interests and help them in the manner they would like during these times. If you're married, you probably promised you'd be by their side "in sickness and in health." So, if you take your promises seriously.........

The Little Things

This section is also directed primarily to men. Today many men do share more of the household tasks than in years past. Yet the majority of women who I've I talk to have said they would appreciate it if their man would help out more around the house. I believe sharing the workload is a valuable practice for couples as it further establishes and reinforces the feeling and spirit of being on the same team, a true partnership in every sense of the word.

It's easy to get in the habit of letting your partner do most of the little things, such as the laundry, the dishes, the shopping, running the kids around, etc. Yet it's also not so difficult to surprise your partner once in while by doing some task that they always handle. Remember, the little things all add up to a lot of work.

A true partnership is one where a couple shares the workload so that neither partner is burdened with all of the chores. Even if you are a man who does help out, there are still always opportunities to do little special things that will continue to express your consideration for your partner. Your lifestyle may dictate some agreed upon delegation of duties. Yet you can still step out of the box that you're both used to once in a while and go beyond the call of duty, which earns major points and makes you feel better about yourself in the process.

Jason has to be at work by 7 a.m. during the week. Since his wife Shelly is just getting out of bed as he leaves the house, it makes sense that she would make the bed. On the weekends however, they usually get up at the same time. He occasionally surprises her by making the bed while she's in the shower. Once in a while he gets up before her and puts on a pot of coffee and makes her breakfast or runs to the store for fresh baked pastries. Shelly truly appreciates the little gestures that Jason makes to be considerate, which encourages him to continue to do them.

The little things are not only easy but great opportunities to continue to show how much you still care about and love your partner.

One night Shelly had to go to a seminar after work. She didr get home until 8:00 p.m. Exhausted, she unlocked the fror door and stepped in out of the rain. To her surprise, Jason had a blanket laid out in front of a crackling fire. He had a special bottle of wine open and some chocolates, fruits, and cheese and crackers. He could see her mood change and the weight of the long day disappear as a beautiful smile came over her face.

A few months can easily slip by without doing anything special for your partner. When you realize it, look for a little way to send the message that you still appreciate and love them. Don't just go and buy flowers as she'll probably wonder what you did wrong that has left you feeling guilty. Instead, do something that makes her life a little easier or more fun! Come home with tickets to a play, San Francisco, or one of her favorite activities. Plan a special date or entire weekend that she doesn't have to do anything but go along for the ride and have fun. Or just do some of the chores she usually handles to make her life a little easier!

You don't always need to buy expensive gifts or make a big romantic production. If you know she's coming home at a certain time, set up some little surprise for her to find, such as doing all the dishes, having a relaxing bubble bath waiting for her complete with candles, or preparing one of her favorite foods. Many of the sweetest gestures are simple and inexpensive, yet show some thought and a little effort were put into doing something nice.

You'd be amazed at how lazy many men get when it comes to even the littlest of things, such as changing the toilet paper. They think "She'll take care of it." True, she probably would. But why not do it yourself?! If you notice that you're almost out of some household items like shampoo, dish soap, milk, and butter - show you want to help by going to the store.

Men, would your wife hate to come home to a vacuumed house or a plate of freshly baked cookies with a note that said how much you still love her? Wash her car for her, or maybe give her a gift certificate for a facial, just because. She'll also notice the little things such as simply picking up after yourself, and it will make a difference in her spirits.

Producing For Your Partner

Imagine throwing a stick to your dog, who fetches the stick and brings it back to you with it's tail wagging. By petting the dog and giving it a treat, you give the dog a "win." Happy and eager to please and receive wins, your dog anxiously awaits another throw of the stick.

Couples can make a game out of doing special things for each other. I call this "producing for each other," which can include doing anything that shows consideration and thoughtfulness. As long as the "producer" receives "wins," they remain eager to please and help out or go the extra mile in the future.

Whether you run to the store to get some popcorn because your partner mentioned they wish they had some, or you fix something of your partner's that's been broken forever, you are producing. If your lover has an upset stomach you can be the hero by driving a few miles to get them some antacid. That is "producing."

Whatever it is that your partner does for you or you for them, the key to having fun and keeping this energy alive is giving and receiving "wins." Wins can be as simple as a genuine thanks, a foot or shoulder rub, or getting your partner their favorite beverage. Too many times the "wins" dry up and are replaced with statements or gestures that express "So what, you merely did your duty." Continue to show your appreciation when your partner produces, which encourages repeat performances and increases the positive energy between a couple.

It's also helpful to ask for a win when your partner overlooks your gestures to help or to be sweet, no matter how small. Women love to nurture and be considerate and men love to be the hero. Give your partner opportunities to win with you. What have you done this week that in some subtle way said, "I still love and appreciate you!?"

~

CHAPTER 22

Partnership Not Ownership
Maintaining individuality while being one as a team

~

Don't Lose Yourself

A partnership is an opportunity for two individuals to participate in life together as a team. When both people respect and appreciate what the other brings to the partnership, they can enjoy feeling the powerful spirit of camaraderie. The partnership is especially strong when both people remain unique individuals, as they were before becoming a couple.

Because most people want their relationship to last, many eventually give up much of who they are in the quest to achieve and maintain peace and harmony. Yet by giving up your freedom of expression in order to not create waves, it's easy to lose your self.

Surely you've heard people say, "I need to find myself" or, "I need to get my life back." Some people have to "adapt" so much to what they think their partner wants them to be like that they are always uncomfortable and they don't feel free to "just be themselves." The reason some people find themselves in this predicament is that they gave up most of who they were in order to be who their partner wanted them to be. For whatever reason they woke up and found themselves living someone else's idea of a life instead of their own.

Many people assess the success of their relationship based upon how much they were able to get their partner to change and become the partner they always wanted. While all of us have been guilty of trying to change our partner to a degree, we must be careful to accept and support our partner in being the unique person we originally fell in love with.

People in relationships need to compromise and adapt to each other. We occasionally need to make some sacrifices for our partner or our families. Yet we don't need to be martyrs. It's a misconception that by sacrificing everything we want and need we will gain the love and respect we desire. On the contrary, a person who loses sight of who they are and what they need and want often loses their partner's respect as well as his/her own identity.

A couple made up of two distinctly different individuals who remain true to themselves is better equipped to experience a mutually satisfying life together. Both will enjoy their lives more fully when together and apart. You're never just someone's spouse. You're the unique, one-of-a-kind person who also happens to be their partner, lover, and friend.

Betty and Ed had been together fifteen years when they came to one of our seminars for a little "tune-up." Throughout the weekend Betty began realizing how she had changed over the years.

Now she wore only the clothes Ed liked her to wear. She never listened to classical music because Ed didn't enjoy it. Before she started dating Ed, Betty used to go dancing, play golf, and go out to dinner with her women friends, but did neither anymore. She grew up in the South, and loved to vacation there when she was single, but had stopped going since Ed didn't like the heat. Betty even gave up the little things such as what they were going to watch on TV and what they would do on their weekends. She always went along with what Ed wanted.

Today they love each other even more since Betty has reclaimed her identity. She feels more alive and happy, and has found that their relationship has grown. Ed respects her more because she's enjoying her favorite activities and more readily expresses her opinions and desires. They have found it easy to compromise.

Both have the freedom to pursue their interests, yet they are still a loving team. Betty is no longer just Ed's shadow.

It's also possible to lose yourself by becoming a martyr to your family. No one can deny that raising children requires an immense amount of time, energy, and focus. But a person who sacrifices everything because they think that's what it takes to be a "good" parent will not lead a very balanced life. The parent who "has no life" other than catering to their family's every want and desire does not necessarily earn the love and respect they may deserve. Children need to see their parents taking care of themselves.

Sometimes both parents lose themselves in the parenting role, ignoring their own relationship for the "sake" of their children. Again this is not necessary or even healthy. A strong couple who takes time out for themselves and nurtures their own relationship will be better equipped to be loving parents. Remember why you came together in the first place, because you love each other and wanted to share life *with each other*. Children are one of the things you may do together as a couple, but are not your sole mission in life. Start at the beginning taking breaks from your child. This doesn't mean you love them any less.

Don't allow yourselves to have just one sole purpose - child rearing. Keep your relationship a priority and everyone will ultimately benefit. Some couples commit a minimum of one weekend a month or one day a week just to being alone, and make certain not to ignore their relationship just because they have children. You have every right and deserve to enjoy life along the way. If you do make time for your relationship and for being alone as individuals instead of being martyrs, you'll be better and more effective parents.

Many older couples say that when their children left home they looked at each other and said, "Now what?" The majority of their lives were consumed by thinking and talking about the children.

Compromise and occasional sacrifice is desirable
and necessary for the longevity of a relationship.
Yet without balance, you can easily lose
what you're working so hard to attain.

Many young couples run into problems with the opposite extreme. No sacrifice, no compromise, no adjustment of lifestyle. Young adults often think the pinnacle of life is achieving independence. But a long-term relationship, and particularly marriage, require consideration of your partner. If you believe you should be able to do anything you want without considering your partner and your relationship, you are destined to have problems. The following is an example from a young couple whom I coached that initially struggled with creating a balance:

> Joel liked to play softball with his buddies. He also liked skiing, hunting, golf, and windsurfing. His interests initially kept keep him pretty busy and never at home with his wife and children. He didn't need to sacrifice all of his interests, but now that he was married with a child he couldn't indulge in all of them as much as he might like to either.
>
> Besides the fact that Joel's wife, Angela, needed help with their son, she also deserved to have some fun. Angela enjoyed bowling with her friends, doing aerobics, and spending time riding her horse. They have worked it out now so that Wednesday night is Joel's night to choose how he wants to spend it, and Angela has Thursday night. They may find other times such as weekends to pursue some of their individual interests, but both have decided to make the remainder of their evenings family nights.
>
> Together they decide as a team what they'll do and where they'll go on their weekends and vacations, and on holidays they alternate whose side of the family they'll visit. No one lives in the other's shadow, and both have ample opportunity to pursue their interests while not doing so at the other's expense. They give each other permission and space to be themselves, and are very considerate in making the effort to both share the parenting and housework so this can be possible.

"Losing yourself" is not always the fault of a partner's unreasonable demands or expectations. Maybe you never stand up for your opinions or ideas, or aren't assertive about what you would like to do. Some people dote after their partner. By seeking to please and nurture, one's partner can be pampered so much they become lazy, enabling them to become demanding and reliant.

Yet regardless of how this loss of one's identity may come about, it's important that a couple does not allow this state of affairs to persist. Both people will benefit by maintaining their own sense of self and individualism, and having the freedom of making choices and having a life that is their own outside of the relationship. If there is any part of you that you feel is important but is being neglected, look for ways to re-establish it in your life.

It is better for the rest of your life to look like
the life you want and deserve than to give it all away
in order to have a relationship without any obstacles.

On A Short String

The direct opposite of the martyr who gives up everything they want for the sake of their partner is the controller. In many historically traditional (and outdated) forms of relationship, one person was in charge. The man typically made the major decisions and was the leader of the tribe. These days, many couples have found it possible and beneficial to have more equal roles.

Each can have a voice in the decisions, share the workload,
be responsible for their roles as parent and partner,
and also be able to direct their own lives.

If a woman wants to go to go back to community college, she should be able to. While it's best to enlist your partner's support, you don't really need their "permission." If a man wants to go hunting for a week every year, he should be able to. He also doesn't need "permission" from his wife. Both are adults and should be able to make decisions such as these for themselves.

Of course, this is only true when both partners are being responsible for their commitments in their relationship, family, and career. A woman need not sit by and watch her husband quit his job, lay around the house, and go off partying with his friends every night - just because he's old enough to run his own life. But if he's been a responsible husband and father and he wants to go hunting, it should be his choice.

You've probably heard the term "I've got him /her on a short leash."
This concept should be abandoned.

Mature couples can deal with each other more like adults than as in a parent-to-child relationship. No one should be parenting the other. This is not to say that parameters shouldn't be established by the couple. On the contrary, parameters are very useful and valuable, *if set together* by the couple, but one person does not need to be in charge. It can and usually does work out better if you approach your life together as a team rather than one of you is the authority and the other their follower.

I've seen situations where men have tried to control their wives' activities and social lives in order to discourage the possibility of any affairs or straying. For example, some men won't "allow" their wives to get a makeover because they are insecure about the strength of their wife's love for them. If she would become more beautiful, other men may become interested. Another classic example of controlling men is when they have discouraged their wife's pursuit of a career so she will remain dependent on him.

There are just as many examples where women try to control their partner's activities and usage of his time. Just like a man can, a woman may try to force her partner to do what she wants by making life very difficult if he doesn't cooperate.

Being on short leash also means that there are usually going to be repercussions for not playing by the others rules, which basically means one person is in control, and the other must obey. This whole way of relating is immature and self-defeating. If you want to boss people around, become a manager. But don't waste your time doing this if you want a truly healthy partnership with the one you love.

If you already have the reins, let go. Give your partner permission to direct their own life, and love them in a manner that has them want to love you back on their own free will. With a solid relationship, once the leash and collar have been taken off, he/she not only wants to stay around, but they also want to play by the rules which you establish together.

As in the chapter on doghouses, all forms of "punishment" should be eliminated. You both lose when someone is being punished. It takes a little more thought and effort, but when someone steps out of line, it is possible to get them to admit to it and take the appropriate measures to see that it doesn't happen again - without punishment. By learning how to communicate and resolve your conflicts in ways mentioned throughout this book, it is possible to create change without force or negativity. Get rid of the stick, and instead motivate with just the carrot. It's not always easy, but it is worth it to undertake this endeavor. Lose the collar and leash, and instead walk side by side as two equals, two friends, two lovers, and two partners.

Partnership - Not Ownership

When we commit ourselves in marriage to spending our lives with another person, we are not taking or giving up ownership. We are creating a team, not bondage. We are choosing to be side by side with our friend. No one has to take the back seat.

To further illustrate this, it used to be that if a man worked for a company that wanted to transfer him, the family just simply went along. *His* career was the priority, and if his wife had a job, she simply had to quit and follow him. If anyone was to stay home and take care of the kids, it was always the woman.

Today the number of dads that have taken on this role is growing significantly, and it has become socially acceptable for him to be Mr. Mom. It *used to be* that in a divorce, women always were awarded the children. Today more women are choosing to not pursue custody, and more men are fighting for it. It's certainly a different world.

It's no longer an unquestioned reality that life simply revolves around the man. There are still people who subscribe to these traditional values and lifestyles, and not just in rural communities and small towns. Some people follow the blueprint of their parents because they want to. Granted, when both partners agree that a man-centered world is what they want, it can work just fine.

Yet what used to work for almost everyone is no longer applicable for many of today's couples. With increased mobility, opportunities, and significant advances towards equality, more and more women in America have come to demand and expect to be considered a partner, not just someone's wife, when it comes to relationships. This translates into all aspects of their life together such as making decisions about how to spend their money, raise their children, where they'll live, and who will do what household tasks.

This of course means that many men, some of who are now divorced or widowed, have to adjust to this new role that many women play. This can be hard for some traditionalists who became used to a wife who tended to go along with almost everything the man wanted. Men who resist this new form of relationship must either find someone with the same set of values, or adjust their expectations accordingly.

Being someone's partner and not just a spouse may mean a radical shift in perspective for some. Many women, after years of submissive participation in marriages, are finding their voice, and speaking up for what they want, need, and hope to have in their lives. Many young women, on the other hand, can't believe there would have ever been any other way than that of equality.

Some partners think they own their husband or wife and should be able to control them by telling them what to do, what to feel, and how to live. They make demands, expect the other to make the sacrifices, and see little reason to compromise. They tend to make little if any effort at making sure their partner feels loved, honored, appreciated, and supported. However, today's relationships are usually more of a partnership than ownership. When you have a "partner," you perceive your arrangement as a team, and it alters the way you treat each other and the expectations that you then have.

This partnership means that you can't sit back on your laurels and get lazy now that your partner has signed on the dotted line. You take care of your body, for yourselves and for each other. You keep life interesting for each other. You support each other's growth, and don't prevent your partner from pursuing new opportunities because they may make a lot of money, get more confidence, or become more attractive - and leave you. Control dissolves and is replaced by partnership, love, and support.

Since the guilt and shame of divorce has gone for many Americans, and women can now take care of themselves and create their own wealth, a man who relies on control or providing the *external* incentives to keep a spouse around is simply using an outdated approach. They must rise to the occasion and give them the love, support, and respect that women want and deserve. No longer will a nice gift or bouquet of flowers suffice in making up for emotional abandonment. Likewise, women can no longer try to "control" their men by telling them what they can and can't do.

Couples can and do get divorced quite easily today, yet, through love instead of force, you can keep your partner interested. It's truly optimal when both partners are equals and both have a say in all matters. This can change the expectations a person has for their partner. Instead of thinking, "My wife must be as I want her to be," a man may think, "This is who my wife is and I must accept and love her for who she is."

We have to provide the incentives to keep our partner interested. This doesn't mean making more money or buying a bigger house, but rather creating a life together that leaves both people feeling honored, valued, respected, and part of a team. Women need to have their material needs met as well as their social, emotional, and physical needs met by their partner. Men who recognize this will be more motivated to be more understanding, more nurturing, more tolerant, more cooperative, more helpful, more romantic, more appreciative, and certainly more affectionate and loving.

This is not a gender issue, though, as both people simply will benefit greatly when they see their union as a team and not a symbol of possession. In every area of life both people can be more like friends, partners, and lovers rather than just someone's husband or wife.

Consider a business partnership, which is usually formed because two people bring to the table a strength or something unique that the other doesn't have. For example, one person may be good at building rapport with people, while the other is good with numbers. Or one may be great working with small details, the other better at visualizing the big picture. They create a partnership because they both recognize that their business will be stronger because of being a team with different skills, abilities, and interests.

Couples' relationships can be very much the same if the perspective is there. Yet too many look at their partner's differences as faults, liabilities, or shortcomings that must be overcome. The differences are what creates a value in being together.

Partners can inspire and support each other's growth, and balance each other. The calm person balances the excitable. The busy person inspires the carefree person to get more done. The sensitive person helps teach the aloof person how to be more involved and connected.

Remember, your relationship can be based upon partnership, not ownership. Consider your partner as your friend, lover, and equal. With the partnership approach, you can expect many more years of healthy cooperation and improved compatibility.

~

Conclusion

A Bridge To The Future

~

Relationships aren't always easy. Most are not without challenge, not without some sacrifice, compromise, occasional disappointments and frustrations. Life is going to have its ups and downs. The strength of a couple can best be measured by how successfully they can weather these storms. When you can create a loving, supportive partnership, relationships are well worth the time and effort they require.

Be quick to resolve conflicts. Strive to be the one to take the initiative to get back to loving each other again promptly! Remember that underneath most of your conflicts, someone is probably not feeling listened to, understood, respected, appreciated, or loved enough. Keep your "emotional bank account" full by lovingly forgiving your partner when they make mistakes. Take responsibility and sincerely apologize for the emotional wounds you inflict.

Look at your upsets as opportunities to grow together and strengthen your partnership. If you both make honest attempts to listen and communicate with each other, you dramatically increase the possibility of overcoming future obstacles that may stand in your way. Instead of installing land mines around "unsafe" subjects, make the effort to build bridges of understanding, compassion, and respect instead.

By eliminating the disapproval, negativity, and messages of "not good enough" in your communications to your partner, you will make major strides in opening the door to increased listening and receptivity to your messages. Be the supportive and open partner who sets an example for those around you. Bring this expressiveness into the intimate part of your relationship, and show your partner through not only your words but also in your presence how much you still care for them.

By accepting and allowing your differences to provide balance to each others lives, your relationship can be the ultimate source of companionship and enjoyment. Express more appreciation and love, and keep looking for the good in each other. Give up trying to change your partner to be more like you. Instead, honor and appreciate your unique perspectives. By finding it easier to laugh at your differences you will become irritated and annoyed less and enjoy life a whole lot more.

Although you'll find there will be times when you will need to be serious and focused on the complexities of life, travel through life together with a lighter load. Make life be more of a fun, pleasant experience instead of a constant challenge. Accept some of life's imperfections and roll with the changes as much as possible. It's especially important to not let your relationship be a constant source of work. Remember to be friends, partners, & lovers. Spontaneity, fun, adventure, laughter, intimacy, and good sex can easily overshadow the serious aspects of life together.

The fundamentals will never change and will always be important; honesty, openness, compromise, respect, sharing, forgiveness, and appreciation. These fundamentals are the pillars upon which the span of the bridge that connects the two of you is supported. Your commitment, love, and determination will strengthen your foundation. Remember, as with your energy, you have the ability to be passionate within you. It is there for you to access when necessary or desired. Only you can bring that inherent passion to life!

Just as a plant requires sunlight and water, your relationship needs to be continually nurtured to keep it healthy and alive. Make your relationship a priority, and continue the effort to keep your partnership interesting & mutually fulfilling. You *can* survive the test of time together!

You might need to occasionally take time out to regroup and evaluate your direction. You, your partner, and your relationship will change. So why not try to direct that change by becoming even more interesting, energetic, and the strongest supporter that your partner has ever had in their life. Endeavor to change and grow *together.* Make these concentrated efforts to keep your partnership not just smoldering, but burning brightly. Inspire each other out of your passion and enthusiasm.

Life is good, and chances are, you've found a pretty incredible person to share your life with. Be the man or woman you would like to say you are. Let go and put both feet in. By doing so you have nothing to lose and everything to gain. Put your heart and soul, your ego and pride, on the line. Do whatever it takes to keep your love alive and have the fulfilling partnership you've always dreamed of.

And thank you for the opportunity to be a contribution to your life. I wish you all of the best in the years to come and a lifetime of passionate partnership!

Note From The Publisher

Thousands of individuals and couples have benefitted from the *"Keeping Love Alive"* seminars which are led by David and Kristin LeClaire. The LeClaire's have also produced an audio tape series for singles titled *"Finding The Right Partner."* To schedule a speaking engagement or for further information about their seminars or tape series, please write or call:

Breaking Thru

1317 N. 78th Street

Seattle, WA 98102

~

1-800-905-1991

~

Free Articles For Relationships In Danger

The following short special interest articles are available
free upon request.
All that is required is having access to a fax machine.

#101 Should We See A Counselor?

#102 Is It Too Late To Save Our Relationship?

#103 The Danger Of Trying To Save A Relationship Via Pregnancy

#104 Message To Your Partner: Are You Going To Do Anything?

#105 Getting Back On Track

#106 Creating A Breakthrough In Your Life!

Call
Breaking Thru
1-800-905-1991

Specify which article(s) you would like,
and we will fax them to you at no charge.
(Due to high demand and expense we can not mail these articles)

Thank you for purchasing "Bridges To A Passionate Partnership."

~